D0085998

The Appreciative Advising Revolution

Jennifer L. Bloom
University of South Carolina

Bryant L. Hutson
University of North Carolina
at Greensboro

Ye He
University of North Carolina
at Greensboro

ISBN 978-1-58874-807-2

Copyright © 2008
Jennifer L. Bloom, Bryant L. Hutson, Ye He

Published by

Stipes Publishing L.L.C.

WINGATE UNIVERSITY LIBRARY

Published by

Stipes Publishing L.L.C.
204 W. University Ave.
Champaign, IL 61820
www.stipes.com
stipes01@sbcglobal.net
Phone 217/356-8391
Fax 217/356-5753

THE APPRECIATIVE ADVISING REVOLUTION

Dedicated To

All Academic Advisors Committed to Optimizing Educational Experiences for Their Students

Acknowledgments

Just like it takes a village to graduate a student, it certainly takes a powerful one to write a book.

First, we would like to acknowledge all our colleagues and friends who have provided continuous support in the development of the Appreciative Advising concept and applications. Since October 2006, we have had the privilege of working with a small but impressive group of colleagues to develop and refine the *Appreciative Advising Instrument*. We have met on a monthly basis via teleconferences, and this group has been instrumental in helping us pilot the instrument as well as fine-tune our thinking on Appreciative Advising: Scott Amundsen, Cathy Buyarski, Phil Christman, Amanda Cuevas, Linda Evans, Joe Murray, Claire Robinson, and Kaye Woodward. Also a number of our friends and colleagues edited the initial draft of this book, and we thank them for their insights, feedback, and suggestions: Katie Beres, Phil Christman, Amanda Cuevas, Jacqui Dozier, Julia Kronholz, Kristi Kuntz, Kathy Rassette, and Robert Ross.

In addition, colleagues from our individual institutions have contributed significantly to the initiation of the Appreciative Advising concept and the development of the Appreciative Advising applications.

Nancy Archer Martin was the co-author of Jenny's first book, *Career Aspirations & Expeditions: Advancing Your Career in Higher Education Administration*, and it was through opportunities to co-present to the American Council on Education's Women's Leadership Forum that Jenny first learned about appreciative inquiry. Teaching her academic advising class at the University of Illinois in 2002 prompted Jenny to co-author with Nancy the article that initiated the Appreciative Advising concept: "Incorporating Appreciative Inquiry into Academic Advising." Therefore, many thanks are due Nancy and the students in Jenny's academic advising class that summer.

Scott Amundsen and Cindra Kamphoff, together with Bryant, led the initial implementation of appreciative inquiry in academic advising at the University of North Carolina at Greensboro (UNCG). An article Scott, Cindra, Bryant, and Julie Atwood published in the *Journal of College Student Retention* reflected the early successful application of Appreciative Advising theory at UNCG. Without their initiative and all the advisors and students who believed in and supported the impact of Appreciative Advising at UNCG, this book would never have been written. Many thanks are extended to all who support Appreciative Advising at UNCG.

We thank all our colleagues who supported us in our daily practice of Appreciative Advising and all the students at our individual institutions whom we have had the privilege to serve. Among those, we would like to give special thanks to Jenny's former colleagues at the University of Illinois at Urbana-Champaign (UIUC): Robbin Burge, Kathy Carlson, Amanda Cuevas, Jim Hall, Judy Kerr, Jim Slauch, Julie Wyant, and Brad Schwartz, the students enrolled in the Medical Scholars Program, the College of Medicine, the Department of Educational Organization & Leadership, the Transition Program, and the Institute of Aviation, as well as pre-med students at UIUC. Jenny also thanks her current colleagues and students in the Higher Education & Student Affairs Program in the Department of Educational Leadership and Policies at the University of South Carolina, especially Christian Anderson, Katie DiSimoni, Gene Luna, Dennis Pruitt, Gordon Southard, and Ken Stevenson.

Likewise, Bryant and Ye thank their colleagues and students at UNCG, especially Tammy Alt, Julie Atwood, Sonja Beach, Kristen Christman, Jennifer Clark, Pat Combs, Brian Davis, Jacqui Dozier, Nannette Funderburk, Jennie Gouker, Micah Martin, Trish Plunkett, Robert Ross, Milvia Sadler, Romia

Smith, Elizabeth Thao, and Steven Yang. All of them helped us develop both professionally and personally, and they serve as constant sources of inspiration and support. Bryant and Ye also thank Terry Ackerman, Deb Bartz, Jewell Cooper, Bert Goldman, Barbara Levin, and James Petersen, examples of outstanding Appreciative faculty advisors who have served as mentors to them both.

All our colleagues in the National Academic Advising Association (NACADA) have also been supportive of us and this project. Thank you to everyone who has attended our presentations at NACADA conferences on this topic over the years. Your questions and insights have helped us further refine our thinking. We also thank the current and past members of the NACADA Board of Directors with whom Jenny has had the pleasure of working over the past 3 years.

We thank our publisher, Ben Watts, of Stipes Publishing in Champaign, Illinois, for believing in us and giving us this opportunity, and we acknowledge the great work that our copy editor, Nancy Vesta, did in clarifying and improving the content of the book.

Lastly, we acknowledge the love and support of our family members and friends. Jenny thanks her husband Steve Sanderson; her parents Gary and Ada Bloom; her brother and his girlfriend, Andrew Bloom and Judy Deverell; her step daughter Kathy Rassette and her husband Matt Rassette; Teri Breitenfeldt; and her aunts, uncles, and cousins. Special thanks go out to the prides and joys of Jenny's life, her grandchildren: Cody Breitenfeldt, Kaitlyn Breitenfeldt, Rachel Rassette, and Rian Rassette.

As a couple, Bryant and Ye would like to jointly thank their parents, Fred and Linda Hutson, and Yixin He and Yao Chen. They would also like to thank their siblings and extended family: Steve, Jami, and Jill Hutson, and Chen He.

Table of Contents

List of Tables and Figures

1. Figures

2. Tables

Section II: Phases of Appreciative Advising

Section III: Applications

Section I:

Introduction and Theoretical Overview

CHAPTER 1

INTRODUCTION

The Appreciative Advising Revolution

Rarely in life does one have the opportunity to participate in a revolution. The Appreciative Advising Revolution is not a bloody uprising against an oppressive government. In this revolution, advisors reexamine themselves and their roles, and they intentionally decide to reframe themselves, their jobs, and the future to better serve students.

The Appreciative Advising Revolution requires courage because delving into this book will be an adventure as seekers are implored to look inward in their efforts to become better advisors outward to students. The way of the revolutionary is difficult. It requires some intense self-examination and some self-questioning. It raises the bar for students and for advisors.

We hope all who open this book are up to the challenge of continuous improvement. This book will not only give Appreciative Advising revolutionaries the theoretical soundness that they seek from the field of academic advising, but it also provides the tools and techniques to transform interactions with students and to impact relationships with others.

The Appreciative Advising Revolution is a grassroots effort. It requires that individuals go against the societal norm of approaching life as a series of problems and instead look at life as a series of opportunities. It requires acknowledgment that even the best advisors can become better advisors. It demands creativity, because advisors do not simply provide a set of prescriptive, lock-step questions to ask or actions to undertake. Finally, it demands leadership. Revolutionaries encounter resistance so they must be resilient to criticism and the pressure to conform. They will be the voice for the new order.

In this book, we ask advisors to raise expectations of themselves and their students, and we point out that success can no longer be defined in terms of student graduation rates. Rather, we define student success as Lipman (1995, pp. 29-30) does:

> Others believe there are many ways to succeed. They believe it is not better to be Picasso than to be Rembrandt, to be Mozart rather than Beethoven.... We each have something unique to offer. To develop it, to offer it clearly, fully, and powerfully—is to succeed. Beethoven did not fail to become another Mozart; he succeeded at becoming Beethoven. Seen this way, success comes from developing your uniqueness. It is rare but not scarce. Every one, potentially, can succeed.

This definition of success requires more work, more energy, more passion, and a new set of techniques that ensure students can reach their full potentials. In this book, we focus on advising for student success as Lipman described. The natural byproducts of this strategy are increased retention and graduation rates.

Contrary to the aggregated reports that colleges generate, students are not numbers: They are people, and advisors know this better than anyone else. Yet, until now, the field of academic advising has not established a coherent framework or package for describing good advising. Yes, theories of advising, CAS standards for advising (Council for the Advancement of Standards in Higher Education, 2005), and best practices articles abound, but a complete framework that marries theory with practice has been missing from advisors' libraries.

This handbook of the revolution provides theory and practical suggestions for implementing Appreciative Advising on individual, unit, and institutional levels. Readers will learn how the University of North Carolina at Greensboro (UNCG) has successfully infused Appreciative Advising throughout its student support programs, including (among others) its University Studies 101 classes, courses for students on probation, and advising of students who have been readmitted. Appreciative Advising offers a complete package for the aspiring revolutionary: It contains theory, practical tools for implementing it, and evidence that it works.

Let the Revolution Begin!

The rallying cry for the Appreciative Advising Revolution is "To be better!" and it means to be better as an advisor, better as a person, and better as a role model. Jim Collins (2001, p. 1) started his best-selling business book with these six words: "Good is the enemy of great." He explained, "We don't have great schools principally because we have good schools. Few people attain great lives, in large part because it is just so easy to settle for a good life.". Student demographics change, the economy cycles, and advisors need to constantly strive to be the lifelong learners that they implore students to become.

We know that many are thinking "This Appreciative Advising appears to involve a lot of work." We can unequivocally say that it does. However, those who adopt the Appreciative Advising mindset and intentionally incorporate the six phases of Appreciative Advising into their work will discover more gratification as an advisor than they had ever thought possible. The work becomes fulfilling in its own right:

> High impact advisors realize that the positive outcomes of advising sessions are not just limited to students; in fact, the real joy of advising occurs when advisors understand how fulfilling it is to really impact other peoples' lives and how much they can learn from their advisees. (Bloom, in press)

Advising as a Profession

Subsequent to the faculty and student affairs professions, academic advising is going through its professionalization period, and advisors are affected much like professional teachers, nurses, and counselors had been throughout the 20th century. One of the strengths of the advising profession is that people come to the field from a wide variety of academic backgrounds. Undergraduate degrees are not awarded in academic advising. Only a few institutions offer graduate-level advising courses, and only recently has the first academic advising master's degree program been established (Kansas State University).

The variety of advisor perspectives can be very healthy for the profession. However, this plurality has a downside: A cohesive description of advising as a discipline is missing from the advising lexicon, and the characterization of a good advisor remains undefined. A comprehensive theory-based and empirically proven conceptualization of advising marks the next step in the professionalization of the field.

The Appreciative Advising model can be a unifying force for the advising profession, which has been flexible enough to incorporate different styles and approaches to advising. Integration is essential not only for academic advisors to establish a professional identity, but also to engage in a common dialogue with faculty and student affairs colleagues. The advising field is at a watershed moment.

In this book, we endeavor to raise to a higher level the dialogue about the characteristics and roles of an academic advisor. We do not claim to provide the panacea for solving every student-related issue. We do, however, present a powerful model of advising as well as evidence that it has been successfully implemented.

The heart and soul of Appreciative Advising is the student. Laing (1967, pp. 62-63) said, "Human beings relate to each other not simply externally, like two billiard balls, but by the relations of the two worlds of experience that come into play when two people meet." Appreciative Advising addresses these concerns by establishing and celebrating a deeper personal relationship between advisors and students through an emphasis on the intrinsic, ontological value of each student encountered.

Purposes of the Book

Numerous articles, reports, and surveys highlight the important role that academic advisors play on today's college campuses. For example, Light (2001, p. 81) stated, "Good advising may be the single most underestimated characteristic of a successful college experience." Similarly, Hossler and Bean (1990) found that in the retention research, academic advising is the most often cited student service in terms of its positive impact on student persistence. De Sousa (2005, p. 1) indicated, "Academic advisors can play an integral role in promoting student success by assisting students in ways that encourage them to engage in the right kinds of activities, inside and outside the classroom."

Given the importance of academic advising and academic advisors, it is surprising to observe the dearth of substantive information on the characteristics that constitute a successful academic advisor or the process to become one. The purpose of this book is to give advisors a set of Appreciative Advising tools to build better rapport with advisees, help students uncover their hopes and dreams, and then co-create a plan for making those dreams come true.

Academic advising efforts typically fall into two major categories: a) individual advising and b) advising programs for special purposes. In this book, we introduce the concept of Appreciative Advising and describe the application of Appreciative Advising in both individual advising sessions and in the development and evaluation of advising programs in higher education settings.

After reading this book, advisors will be able to

1. identify their advising strengths and purposes;

2. recognize that advising is much more than helping students select classes for next semester;

3. have more confidence in their ability to positively impact students' lives;

4. understand and appreciate the important contributions advisors make to the campus community;

5. attain greater knowledge regarding the principles of Appreciative Advising;

6. incorporate Appreciative Advising principles and practices in advising sessions;

7. build stronger rapport with students;

8. ask positive, open-ended questions that elicit stories from students, which will serve as the foundation of their academic and personal achievements;

9. measure the effectiveness of advising sessions;

10. identify strategies for implementing Appreciative Advising;

11. identify and understand how to leverage resources in the campus environment to achieve Appreciative change; and

12. develop and evaluate programs by incorporating Appreciative Advising principles to better serve a wide range of student populations in higher education settings.

Organization of the Book

This book is divided into four different sections. Section I contains this introduction as well as the theoretical underpinnings and the history of Appreciative Advising (Chapter 2). Those who may be wary of, or intimidated by, theory will especially appreciate Chapter 2 because it emphasizes the theory-to-practice aspects of each theory we mention.

Section II is in many ways the heart and soul of the book. In this section the six phases of Appreciative Advising are discussed. Chapter 3 provides an overview, and it is followed by a chapter devoted to each phase: Disarm (Chapter 4), Discover (Chapter 5), Dream (Chapter 6), Design (Chapter 7), Deliver (Chapter 8), and Don't Settle (Chapter 9). In each of these chapters, we discuss key features of each phase, offer an example of an advising interaction at each stage, and provide specific ideas for implementing each phase (we call these discussions the "Tool Box").

Section III focuses on current actual Appreciative Advising–based programmatic initiatives (Chapter 10) as well as specific advice on how to develop and administer programs (Chapter 11). Chapter 12 introduces steps on how to evaluate Appreciative Advising programs established on campus.

Section IV is the conclusion. We offer specific suggestions on how to initiate the implementation of Appreciative Advising on campus (Chapter 13).

CHAPTER 2

THEORETICAL FRAMEWORK OF APPRECIATIVE ADVISING

Appreciative Advising Defined

Appreciative Advising is a social-constructivist advising philosophy that provides a framework for optimizing advisor interactions with students in both individual and group settings. Embracing the Appreciative mindset, advisors intentionally use positive, active, and attentive listening and questioning strategies to build trust and rapport with students (Disarm); uncover students' strengths and skills based on their past successes (Discover); encourage and be inspired by students' stories and dreams (Dream); co-construct action plans with students to make their goals a reality (Design); support students as they carry out their plans (Deliver); and challenge both themselves and their students to do and become even better (Don't Settle).

The principles of Appreciative Advising are enriched by a diverse set of theories and a wealth of research. This chapter focuses on how Appreciative Advising melds theory into practice.

Academic Advising Theories

In 1972, two separate seminal articles on advising were penned by Burns Crookston and Terry O'Banion, who were the first to suggest that academic advising involved more than helping students schedule classes. O'Banion (1994/1972) posited that advisors should initiate advising with an exploration of students' life and career goals before discussing majors, classes, and course schedules. Crookston (1994/1972) exploded the myth that advising should be strictly prescriptive; that is, he said it should not be a process in which advisors simply tell students the actions to take and expect obedient compliance from them. Although this straightforward approach can help students get through a course of study quickly, information only flows one way (Church, 2005; Lowenstein, 1999). As a result, prescriptive advising does not encourage students to reflect upon the ways that a course of study impacts their development or aligns with their career and life goals.

Crookston (1994/1972) contrasted prescriptive advising with developmental advising, which focuses on the development of the student and the formation of career goals, values, and decision-making ability. However, *developmental advising* has been a broad term often used to merely describe good advising practices. As Matthew Church (2005) observed, developmental advising practice is generally based on the assumption that students lack goals and decision-making skills. In addition, most developmental models assert that the advisor is the source of appropriate values. Furthermore, developmental advising does not necessarily encourage academic mentoring, which is particularly important to the relationship between faculty members and students.

In 1999, Mark Lowenstein argued that neither a prescriptive nor developmental lens would be as effective as an academically centered vision. Academically centered advising facilitates the student's ability to interact with and benefit from institutional academic programs, course sequencing, and complementary course scheduling. Advisors taking the academically centered approach aim to give advisees the tools for lifelong learning (Church, 2005; Lowenstein, 1999). Through this model, the advisor purposely supports students in developing interests in learning and academic achievement. However, a student with a highly developed love for learning does not necessarily know how to align that passion with a career. Also in 1999, Martha Hemwall and Kent Trachte critiqued developmental advising while bringing forth a new approach to advising called "praxis," which involves the use of critical self-reflection to help students connect their learning to institutional mission.

Later, E. R. Melander (2002) described student-centered advising, an approach that aids the student in developing the skills and behaviors needed to become successful via the total college experience. The student-centered advising merges the curricular and the social aspects of college to allow for holistic development. However, under this theory, students take primary responsibility for their academic and career development, which some may be unready to do until relatively late in their course of study.

Confusion over the definitive practice and appropriate theory of academic advising has been bewildering to many and possibly even detrimental to professionals and the field. Moreover, none of the theories presents specific, practical tools for implementation.

Appreciative Advising is not only built on a strong, theoretical underpinning, but it also arms academic advisors with an arsenal of tools that will allow them to translate theory into practice. Appreciative Advising helps students capitalize and make meaningful their collegiate academic and extracurricular opportunities and experiences.

Appreciative Advising is a reciprocal approach to advising where both the student and the advisor benefit and learn. Figure 2-1 depicts this synergy between the student, the advisor, and the advising content. The ultimate goal of Appreciative Advising is beyond the advising content itself. It leads to a change of perspective for both advisors and students.

Figure 2-1. The reciprocal advising process

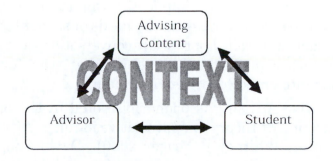

Theories that Inform Appreciative Advising

Appreciative Advising draws upon a wide range of theories from the organizational development, student development, teaching pedagogy, and counseling realms. We will briefly discuss how these theories impact Appreciative Advising.

Appreciative Advising originated from the discipline of positive psychology, which is the study of optimal human functioning and the "strengths and virtues that enable individuals and communities to thrive" (Positive Psychology Center, 2008). Instead of being focused on the negative aspects of human functioning, positive psychology is based on a wellness model and is used to explore mental health promotion and wellness. With an emphasis on the inquiry into human goodness and excellence, positive psychology is the scientific study of the affirming developmental and situational stops between birth and death (Peterson, 2006).

Abraham Maslow (1954) introduced and discussed the importance of positive psychology in the last chapter of his book *Motivation and Personality*. In 1998, President of the American Psychological Association, Martin Seligman, advocated that the members of the organization devote more time and energy to understanding the importance of positive emotions, wellness, and empowering relationships (Stickel & Callaway, 2007). Increasingly, research findings indicate that positive psychology and wellness strategies foster healthy human development (Snyder & Lopez, 2007). Positive psychology also can be employed to implement strategies for institutional change that can impact both the system and the individuals within it (Peterson, 2006). Therefore, it holds important implications for academic advisors, who are charged with addressing the needs of students through intentional and culturally appropriate conversations and through developing programs and relationships that transform their institutions into empowering environments.

Appreciative Advising is primarily rooted in the organizational development theory of appreciative inquiry (AI) (Cooperrider, Sorenson, Whitney, & Yeager, 2000). David Cooperrider, while a doctoral student at Case Western Reserve University, first developed the AI model as a means to engage people across a system in renewal, change, and focused performance (Cooperrider, 1990). AI is based on the premise that organizations should build upon their strengths rather than efforts to fix weaknesses. As stakeholders in the organization share their stories of individual and organizational success, they begin to identify and make meaning of the organization's strengths. Cooperrider and Diane Whitney (2000, p. 10) defined AI as "the cooperative search for the best in people, their organizations, and the world around them.... AI involves the art and practice of asking questions that strengthen a system's capacity to heighten positive potential." It mobilizes inquiry through the construction of "unconditional positive questions" and provides all participants with a voice in creating the future of the organization.

In addition to the AI model, those practicing Appreciative Advising utilize principles of reality therapy to consider the context of advising interactions. Reality therapy is a counseling technique based on choice theory through which people are taught ways to direct their own lives, make effective choices, and develop the strength to handle life stresses and problems. According to choice theory, individuals can choose and control their own behavior to satisfy their needs (Glasser, 1986, 2000).

In William Glasser's (1986) view, behavior is totally comprised of four inseparable components: acting, thinking, feeling, and physiology. Even if one is feeling very low or one's physiology is in an unhealthy state, the individual can still choose to change the more accessible components of behavior (i.e., acting or thinking) and thus improve the situation. When applied to the counseling process, reality therapy places a great deal of importance on the relationship between the client and the counselor. Glasser calls this "involvement." Similarly, in the Appreciative Advising process, the advisor builds relationships with students to keep them engaged in exploring the multiple avenues for meeting their needs. Advisors are also sensitive to the unique needs of individual students.

Appreciative Advising is also influenced by Martin Covington's (1992) self-worth theory, which states that students strive for academic achievement out of the need to protect their sense of worth or personal value. Several factors influence a student's sense of worth, including performance level, self-estimates of ability, and the degree of effort expended. A student's perceived self-worth is highly dependent on accomplishments. The implication of this linkage is that unless students can become successful at some valued activity, they will be cut off from a major source of self-esteem.

According to Covington (1992), self-perception of ability has both a direct and an indirect influence on self-worth. The direct link demonstrates that the mere perception of high ability can sometimes imply worthiness even in the absence of accomplishments. However, an individual's sense of worth cannot long rest solely on a reputation for intelligence. Therefore, the ability-performance–self-worth linkage indicates that a combination of ability and performance is necessary to maintain a sense of worthiness. In K-12 settings, teachers tend to reinforce the value of trying and thus create for the student the linkage between effort and self-worth. However, performance is needed to maintain this feeling of worthiness (Covington, 1992). Appreciative Advisors understand that motivation to achieve tends to peak when institutional expectations and student beliefs about ability and personal strengths align. They also believe that through positive questioning, academic advisors can assist students in identifying these strengths and aligning them with their future life and career goals as well as with institutional expectations.

Viewing advising as a reciprocal process and taking the advising context into consideration, Appreciative Advisors utilize social constructivist theory to provide concrete advising strategies that guide the advising process. The understanding that new knowledge is constructed based on prior knowledge and learning is gained through personal experiences and social interactions constitutes the essence of social constructivist theory.

Recognizing the socially constructed nature of learning, Lev Vygotsky (1978) emphasized the importance of culture, language, and context in the knowledge-construction process. Cooperation and mutual respect in social interactions are critical aspects of Vygotsky's theory. Two key concepts from Vygotsky impact Appreciative Advising: the zone of proximal development (ZPD) and scaffolding. ZPD depicts the gap between a person's actual development level and his/her potential level of development. When both advisor and advisee engage in cooperative learning, such as in Appreciative Advising, the outcome is determined by the social interaction and collaborative problem solving between the student and the advisor. That is, the student progresses and achieves more in Appreciative Advising (thus minimizing the ZPD) than she/he would enjoy outside of a relationship with a knowledgeable advisor. At the same time, the advisor benefits from expansion of his/her scope of knowledge.

Through Vygotsky's (1978) scaffolding, the Appreciative Advisor initially provides more support and infrastructure at the beginning of the process (Bloom, in press; Bloom, Cuevas, Evans, & Hall, 2007), but then she/he artfully removes the scaffolding over time to facilitate further growth and development as the student builds self-confidence and knowledge. Eventually the scaffolding is completely dismantled and the student graduates with a sense of direction and ability.

Figure 2-2, the Appreciative Advising theoretical framework, visually demonstrates how previously established theories have guided the development of the Appreciative Advising model. AI distinguishes Appreciative Advising as a positive and generative process. Choice theory influences how Appreciative Advisors consider student needs and the advising context. Social constructivist theory informs Appreciative Advising strategies that serve as scaffolds in the advising process. The elements of the theoretical framework support the meaningful partnerships between the advisor and the student as well as the co-creation and development of individualized strategies and tools that characterize Appreciative Advising.

Figure 2-2. Appreciative advising theoretical framework

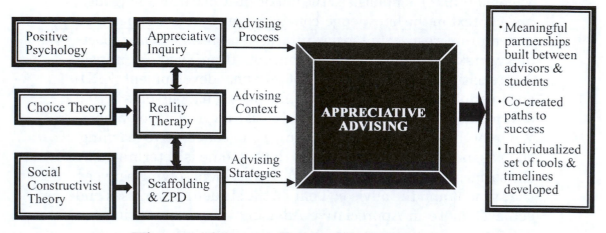

History of Appreciative Advising

Jennifer Bloom and Nancy Martin (2002) were the first to draw parallels between AI and academic advising by demonstrating how the four phases of AI could be used to enhance advisors' interactions with students. The Student Academic Services Office at UNCG subsequently transformed the concept into practice (Hutson & Atwood, 2006; Hutson, Amundsen, & He, 2005; Hutson, He, & Amundsen, 2006; Kamphoff, Hutson, Amundsen, Atwood, 2007). In his doctoral dissertation on UNCG's academic recovery programs, Bryant Hutson (2006) extended the application of Appreciative Advising by describing intake and recovery models for Appreciative Advising and by measuring the positive impact of Appreciative Advising on student academic achievement.

Practitioners of Appreciative Advising and AI focus on creating affirmative change by asking positive, open-ended questions that elicit stories. Through narrative sharing, they solicit and emphasize positive emotions (Fredrickson, 2001, 2006) as well as generate positive intent (Bushe, 1995). In the past few years, advising personnel at several postsecondary institutions, such as Eastern Illinois University, Eastern Kentucky University, Indiana University–Purdue University Indianapolis, Miami University–Hamilton campus, The University of Illinois at Urbana-Campaign (UIUC), and The University of South Carolina (USC) have adopted Appreciative Advising. These professionals have contributed significantly to the refinement of Appreciative Advising through their work with students and through discussions of their practices at local, regional, and national conferences.

Based on the review of other advising professionals' work and our own discussion, we define Appreciative Advising as a social-constructivist advising philosophy that provides an advising framework for advisors to use in optimizing their interactions with students in both individual and group settings. In addition to theoretical perspectives, Appreciative Advising also draws from various other disciplines. For example, because of the one-on-one nature of the typical advising session and advisors' role in facilitating students' decision making, aspects from the intentional interviewing model (Ivey & Ivey, 2007) inform Appreciative Advising.

Allen Ivey and Mary Ivey (2007) proposed a microskills hierarchy to address the fundamental communication skills needed for intentional interviewing in counseling, where interviewers develop their microskills based on their understanding of ethics, multicultural competence, and wellness. While much of the model applies specifically to interviewing in a counseling setting, two early stages, attending behavior and basic listening skills, fit the goals of Appreciative Advising. Attending behavior is characterized by positive nonverbal and key paralinguistic features in interaction and communication: eye contact, body language, vocal qualities, and verbal tracking. Listening skills, including questioning, observing, paraphrasing, and reflecting, are inherent to attending behavior (Ivey & Ivey, 2007).

Drawn upon the understanding of various theories and principles, the basic assumptions of Appreciative Advising can be summarized as follow:

1. Every college student has the potential for academic success.

2. Each college student possesses unique strengths.

3. Through explorations of their backgrounds, past experiences, present status and relationships, and future goals and dreams, students can identify sources of their own strengths.

4. In their quest to be academically successful, students must identify and build upon their strengths.

5. Not all college students have identified their strengths or the strategies necessary to utilize and develop these strengths.

6. Advisors play an important role in every college student's journey to optimize his/her educational experiences and enhance his/her self-knowledge.

7. The interactions between advisors and students will impact both the advisors' and the students' thoughts, viewpoints, and behaviors.

8. Advisors must be aware of how their own perspectives, attitudes, and language impact the advisor-student relationship.

These assumptions may appear to be common sense, but they describe an entirely different advising relationship than is characterized by other models. Assumptions 2, 3, and 4, for example, mirror constructivist theory: Knowledge is constructed based on prior knowledge and learning is gained through experience. Diversity among students requires advisors to be prepared to individualize their questions for and interactions with each student. Assumptions 6, 7, and 8 illustrate the roles and responsibilities of the academic advisor and also reframe advising as an innovative and reciprocal learning process for both advisors and students.

Summary

A wide array of theoretical constructs forms the theoretical infrastructure of Appreciate Advising. Informed by positive psychology, choice theory, and social constructivist theory, Appreciative Advising uniquely blends appreciative inquiry, reality therapy, scaffolding, and the ZPD.

Section II:

Phases of Appreciative Advising

CHAPTER 3

APPRECIATIVE ADVISING OVERVIEW AND THE APPRECIATIVE ADVISING MINDSET

Appreciative Advising Overview

The literature indicates a variety of AI models. Most of them involve four phases, which sometimes carry different names. The two main models are known as the "Four-D" and the "Four-I" (Watkins & Mohr, 2001). Diana Whitney and Amanda Trosten-Bloom (2003, p. 6) described the Four-D model in these terms:

- Discover—Appreciate what is.

- Dream—Imagine what might be.

- Design—Determine what should be.

- Destiny—Create what will be.

The Four-I model is defined by Initiate, Inquire, Imagine, and Innovate phases. In the Initiate stage, one is introduced to and selects a topic. The Inquire phase involves creating the questions that will be asked in the Imagine phase in which interview data are gathered and a vision is established. At the Innovate stage, people commit to carrying out the vision (Watkins & Mohr, 2001).

When we started infusing appreciative inquiry into our academic advising, we found that the Four-D was a better match than the Four-I for our interactions with students. However, as we continued to refine and update the Appreciative Advising model, the traditional Four-D model proved insufficient to fully describe our advising processes. First, we did not like the name of the "Destiny" phase because it seemed to imply that the stars dictated whether one could successfully implement the plan set forth in the Design phase. To reflect students' command of their own destinies and their responsibility to act upon the plan created in the Design phase, we prefer "Deliver" for this stage.

Second, the 4-D Model did not sufficiently address the importance of our very first meetings with students. The first impression advisors make with students establishes the students' level of trust and dictates the stories they will share. Because this stage is so critically important, we named it "Disarm" and positioned it to precede the other phases. Although it was added later to the Appreciative Advising model itself, it is the first phase employed when meeting with students.

We also were concerned that our Deliver phase did not adequately convey the importance of challenging students to raise their own expectations for themselves. Therefore, we identified the sixth phase of Appreciative Advising as Don't Settle.

The six stages of Appreciative Advising model have unique features. In the Disarm phase of the Appreciative Advising model, practitioners strive to make a positive first impression with students and allay any fear or suspicion the students might have of meeting with the advisor. In the Discover phase, the Appreciative Advisor continues to build rapport with students and learns about their strengths, skills, and abilities. Uncovering students' hopes and dreams for their futures characterizes the Dream phase. Once Appreciative Advisors know advisees' dreams, they can spend time in the Design phase co-creating a plan to meet those aspirations. The students carry out their plan in the Deliver stage, which is the time that the Appreciative Advisor supports them as they encounter roadblocks. In the final phase, Don't Settle, Appreciative Advisors challenge students to achieve their full potential.

The Appreciative Advising Mindset

Although six phases comprise its infrastructure, Appreciative Advising is not a lock-step process for working with students. Instead, the Appreciative Advisor employs creativity to build rapport with students, decipher their hopes and dreams, and assist them with designing and implementing a plan to accomplish their goals. To unleash each person's unique story and potential, the advisor must be steeped in the Appreciative Advising mindset.

The first component of the Appreciative Advising mindset embodies caring about and believing in the potential of each student. Although the potential for each student may not be completely obvious, the Appreciative Advisor always strives to "see the extraordinary in the ordinary" (Jones, 1999). To do this, he/she must believe in the goodness of the advisee and treat him/her like one would want a close relative to be treated by an advisor (Bloom & Martin, 2002). An anonymous wise person penned the phrase, "The people who make a difference in your life are not the ones with the most credentials, the most money, or the most awards. They are the ones who care." Advisors must care enough about each student that they are willing to devote and focus their time, attention, and training to help each and every student optimize her/his abilities and talents.

The term "Appreciative" in this context has two meanings. The advisor esteems the student's capacities and strengths; this type of appreciation should be embedded in an advisor's professionalism. Additionally, Appreciative Advisors guide students to uncover and appreciate their own unique strengths and passions. Therefore, Appreciative Advising is perhaps the best example of a fully student-centered approach.

Second, the Appreciative Advising mindset creates an attitude of gratefulness: The Appreciative Advisor realizes his/her fortune at having the opportunity to positively impact other peoples' lives and the future of the country. According to B. Joseph White, President of the University of Illinois, "Education is the most powerful means of increasing individual opportunity and creating more prosperous, fairer, and more just societies. So to have the privilege of participating in that mission is as much as anybody could hope for in life" (Reiter, 2005, p. 21).

We truly believe that we are honored to work in higher education as academic advisors because there can be no better business than helping people achieve their hopes and dreams. We also acknowledge the difficulty of orchestrating meaningful sessions with students in a 30 minute (or shorter) appointment from 8 to 5 every day for weeks on end, especially right before and during registration periods. All advisors must constantly remind themselves of the privilege and responsibility that has been bestowed upon them.

Every day, academic advisors pay homage to all of the people who assisted them throughout their lives. The 19th-century philosopher, George Adams (2008), said

> There is no such thing as a "self-made" man. We are made up of thousands of others. Everyone who has ever done a kind deed for us, or spoken one word of encouragement to us, has entered into the make-up of our character and of our thoughts, as well as our success.

While no one can pay back others for their belief and support, an academic advisor can pay it forward through their work with students. The movie *Pay it Forward* (McLagen & Treisman, 2000) is about an eighth grade student who receives a class assignment to think of an idea that would change the world. The student's idea was to do one nice thing for three people with no expectation for repayment except that the beneficiary would be obligated to do nice things for three other people. The student practiced his philosophy and he ended up positively impacting the world. The advisor gets paid to pay it forward every day!

Short of impacting the whole world, the giving creates a larger picture in which helping others reaps benefits outside the individual beneficiaries. Not only is giving the professionally sound and socially conscientious action, it may benefit the giver in a very concrete way. As is pointed out in the book, *The Pact*,

> People should give even if they are selfish because
> there are selfish reasons to give. Your gift might touch
> the life of a kid who otherwise might end up breaking
> into your house, jacking your car, or selling drugs to
> your child. Or your gift might help to raise the brain
> surgeon who someday saves your life. I'm not trying to
> scare anyone, but the point is that there is no excuse not
> to give, even if your reason is a selfish one. But there is
> another selfish reason to give: when you give to someone
> else, I've found, surprisingly, that you often receive
> as well. (Davis, Jenkins, & Hunt, 2002, pp. 137-38)

The third component of the Appreciative Advising mind-set is the acknowledgment that no matter how many awards earned or thank you notes received from students, an advisor can always become better at the craft. Appreciative Advisors are continually refining their questioning and listening skills as they proactively seek feedback from students to improve their advising technique. George Kuh, the professor behind the National Survey of Student Engagement, calls this continued fine-tuning "positive restlessness" (Kuh, Kinzie, Schuh, & Whitt, 2005). Appreciative Advisors are constantly promoting the importance of lifelong learning and thus lead by example and continually seek to improve their own advising.

Sometimes when we present on the topic of Appreciative Advising, people will say to us, "I want to do Appreciative Advising, but it seems like kind of a waste because the culture on our campus is very student-unfriendly. So why should I bother?" We reply that while an individual may have no control over the culture outside of the office, the advisor does control what happens in her/his individual meetings with students. Advisors possess the power to create what Collins (2007) calls a "pocket of greatness." Just because others do not understand or buy into the Appreciative Advising model, an advisor can and should implement this model in individual appointments with students. Change happens one person at a time, and we encourage advisors to take the lead and provide an example of greatness in advising.

As the impact on students becomes apparent over time, others on campus will follow those who lead with the Appreciative Advising model.

Remembering the amount of power an advisor holds characterizes the fourth component of the Appreciative Advising mindset. Oftentimes, professional academic advisors feel that they are at the bottom of the university administrative food chain. Regardless of whether that perception is true or not on any particular campus, advisors must remember that they serve students and are therefore some of the most important people at the institution.

Advisors must choose to use their power for good and not for evil. This means that advisors should be careful not to inadvertently crush a student's dream through a misspoken word or thoughtless action. Maya Angelou (2006) said, "I've learned that people will forget what you said, people will forget what you did, but people will never forget how you made them feel." Everyone wants to feel important and respected.

> Always remember this one important fact: every person you meet is wearing a sign around his or her neck that very few people know how to read. The sign has only four words on it, but 95 percent of those competing for the business don't have a clue as to what is says. The four words are "Help me feel important" (West & Anthony, 2005, p. 8).

Those with an Appreciative Advising mindset are truly interested in students and enjoy learning from them. The adversity that students have overcome, their accomplishments, and their inspirational stories continue to amaze the Appreciative Advisor. However, to be inspired by students, advisors must hear students' stories, and thus they must become adept at eliciting student narratives. Asking positive, open-ended questions is the hallmark of Appreciative Advising and illustrates caring, the fifth component of the mindset. To ask great questions, Appreciative Advisors need "a deep-seated, insatiable, absolutely have-to-know, fanatical curiosity" (West & Anthony, 2005, p. 13). Asking great questions and hearing students' stories comprise the best antidote to advisor burnout because no two students' stories are the same.

The sixth component of the Appreciative Advising mindset consists of cultural awareness and responsiveness in interactions with students. To understand and communicate with others, individuals first need to explore and understand their own cultural identity. All cultural aspects of life, such as class, ethnicity and race, gender, exceptionality, religion, language, and age impact personal worldviews and determine behavior.

Everyone belongs to multiple subcultural groups simultaneously (e.g., a middle-aged, middle-class, White female Christian; a young, college-educated, African American businessman, etc.). To be effective when interacting with students, advisors not only need to reflect on their own cultural identities and be aware of the existence of various cultural norms, but they also need to treat everyone in a culturally sensitive manner. Adapting from Geneva Gay's (2000) definition of culturally responsive teaching, we put forth the concept of culturally responsive academic advising: utilizing knowledge of self, cultural aspects, students, procedures, and content in specific higher education settings to facilitate student academic growth and cultural identity development. Similar to culturally responsive teachers (Gay, 2000), culturally responsive advisors

- acknowledge the legitimacy of the cultural heritages of different cultural groups, both as legacies that affect students' dispositions, attitudes, and approaches to academic development and as assets that lead to student cultural-identity development.

- build bridges of meaningfulness between home and institutional experiences as well as between academic abstractions and lived sociocultural realities.

- use a wide variety of advising strategies that are connected to different learning styles and learning needs.

- facilitate students' ability to know and praise their own and others' cultural heritages.

- incorporate multicultural information, resources, and materials in advising sessions and advising programs.

Enhancing cultural knowledge and embracing the Appreciative mindset enable advisors to achieve cultural awareness. Without the cultural knowledge, advisors will be unable to build upon student cultural assets. Without the Appreciative mindset, incomprehensive cultural knowledge may lead to stereotypes and subsequent prejudice and bigotry. The Appreciative Advising techniques and questions featured throughout this book will enable advisors to be culturally responsive in their interactions with students and continue their development as culturally responsive advisors.

In summary, the six components of Appreciative Advising are

- caring about and believing in the potential of each student.

- appreciating the good fortune to positively impact other peoples' lives and the future of society.

- acknowledging that one can always become better at her/his craft (i.e., positive restlessness).

- remembering the amount of power students perceive advisors to possess and reflecting on how to best utilize that power.

- being truly interested in students and enjoying learning from them.

- being culturally aware and responsive in interactions with students.

Developing an Appreciative Advising mindset is an important prerequisite to becoming an Appreciative Advisor. This shift in the approach to advising and advisees generates powerful change, but it is not always an easy shift to make. Most are trained from a very early age to look for problems and to have a deficit-based mentality, so questions such as "What is wrong?" "How can I fix it?" "What can we do to prevent this from happening again?" constitute most inquiries into life.

Embracing an Appreciative Advising mindset, one asks "What is going right here?" "How can we do more of this?" The questions sound simple, but they represent a major paradigm shift that takes time to develop. Reflection and thoughtfulness on a daily basis, including a need to be cognizant of the manner in which they speak about students and parents to a colleague, allow advisors to see how a mindset translates into behavior. After adopting the Appreciative Advising mindset advisors will enjoy the positive effects on relationships with students and also with friends, family members, and loved ones. The Appreciative Advising mindset puts in motion powerful changes and we urge advisors to embrace it today!

In the following six chapters, we discuss in detail the features of the six phases of Appreciative Advising. We provide advising examples utilizing Appreciative Advising in practice and explore the strategies that can be used in Appreciative Advising sessions. See Table 3-1 for an overview of Appreciative Advising by stage.

Table 3-1. Overview of key Appreciative Advising features by stage

Appreciative Advising Stages	Key Features	Tool Box
Disarm	1: Warm welcome 2: Safe and comfortable environment 3: Appropriate self-disclosure 4: Appropriate nonverbal behavior	Self-reflection Generate one's own narratives in advising
Discover	5: Effective open-ended questioning 6: Attending behavior and active listening 7: Strength-based story reconstruction	Appreciative Advising Inventory Appreciative Advising questions Note-taking strategies Buckingham's (2007b) *Trombone Player Wanted*
Dream	8: Creating powerful images 9: Prospective framework for dreaming 10: Making purposeful connections between the Dream and Discover phases	Guided imaging Interview Four-corner index cards
Design	11: Teach students how to make decisions 12: Provide positive feedback 13: Be aware of the curse of knowledge 14: Making effective referrals	Backward designing Graphic organizers Personal presidential cabinet Glossary list for academic advising Victim/creator language
Deliver	15: Energizing students to be their best 16: Academic hope 17: Ending the conversation well 18: Following up	Follow up Questions to close the meeting with students
Don't Settle	19: Challenge and support 20: Raising the bar 21: Virtuous cycle	Appreciative Advising rubric Personal success letters Simple truths web slideshow

CHAPTER 4

THE DISARM PHASE

Disarm: To overcome or allay the suspicion, hostility, or antagonism of.[1]

Disarm

Recognizing the importance of first impressions, we conceptualized the Disarm phase as the initial creation of a safe, welcoming environment for students. "Initial encounters are emotionally concentrated events that can overwhelm us…. We walk away from them with a first impression that is like a Polaroid picture—a head-to-toe image that develops instantly and never entirely fades" (Flora, 2004). People need only 3 seconds to make judgments about others; for early humans, who needed to almost instantaneously decide if someone posed a threat, the skill proved invaluable in life-and-death situations (Flora, 2004). To garner trust, advisors must make a positive first impression on advisees.

Whenever people meet for the first time, the interaction is never neutral: It will be perceived negatively or positively by all parties (Rath & Clifton, 2004). This initial interaction is an exchange based on language, and the words chosen to use—whether positive or negative—set the tone for the relationship. In other words, the first question precipitates the nature of the relationship.

---

[1] www.dictionary.com

Key Appreciative Advising Feature 1: Warm Welcome

Jeanette Henderson and Roy Henderson (2007) stated that every interaction begins with an acknowledgment. They purported that acknowledgment starts with a full frontal stance, which "requires that both parties turn their entire bodies to face one another, shoulders squared up, looking at each other straight in the eye" (p. 15). When persons avoid acknowledgment, such as by looking down at the floor when a stranger enters an elevator, no interaction begins. However, meetings initiated with a full frontal stance clearly signal a desire to engage with the other party.

Other research indicates that a smile is the best way to create a positive first impression. Upon initial meetings, people first search each other's faces for a smile; "We can pick up a smile from 30 meters away," says Paul Ekman, professor of psychology at the University of California Medical School in San Francisco and a pioneer on research on facial expressions (as cited in Flora, 2004). "A smile lets us know that we're likely to get a positive reception, and it's hard not to reciprocate" (Flora, 2004).

The Appreciative Advisor puts together the full frontal stance with the smile and a warm welcome: "Hi Monica, my name is Jenny, and I am glad you came in to see me. Please follow me to my office." Jenny continues facing Monica, shakes her hand warmly, looks her in the eye, and uses her name early and often throughout the conversation. If Jenny had met Monica in a reception area for students, she certainly would have walked out to meet Monica in the reception area, where she would have greeted her and escorted her to Jenny's office. This welcoming gesture, which engenders a more friendly approach than a receptionist's point down the hall to the office, sends the clear message to Monica, and the other students in the reception area, that Jenny values and respects her.

Key Appreciative Advising Feature 2:
Safe and Comfortable Environment

The Appreciate Advisor's office should be clean and welcoming. Distractions should be minimal: Cell phones and the audio cue that announces new e-mail should be turned off. The advisee should be offered a comfortable and attractive seat where he/she will not feel physically trapped. The advisee should be looking at an attractive space and should not need to squint from the sunlight blaring through a window. To see the view that the advisee will see, the advisor should sit in the chair typically used by the students and judge the comfort level of that seat.

Key Appreciative Advising Feature 3:
Appropriate Self-disclosure

Appreciative Advisors decorate their offices such that visitors get acquainted with them and their interests. A display of select personal items allows students to make an early connection with the advisor. For example, Jenny's walls feature items meaningful to her: a picture of her and Michael Jordan, a Wheaties box with the 1990 Cincinnati Reds World Champions on it, a picture from her former institution, among other personal memorabilia. Inevitably, students ask her immediately about the Michael Jordan picture.

Many students initially feel intimidated by advisors, and a warmly and personally decorated office communicates that the resident advisor is a human. In the K-12 system, a trip to the counselor's office often indicated that the student was in trouble. As a result, the Appreciative Advisor may need to help students overcome years of anxiety about going to the "counselor's office." If advisors are unsuccessful in demonstrating that they are friendly, students will likely perceive advisors as intimidating authority figures. Advisees arrive guarded, and during the Disarm phase, the Appreciative Advisor takes the responsibility to make them feel comfortable.

Key Appreciative Advising Feature 4: Appropriate Nonverbal Behavior

During the Disarm phase, the Appreciative Advisor conveys an interest in students. The phrase, "Don't sweat the small stuff," doesn't apply for Appreciative Advisors because they understand that little cues make a big difference on the student's first impression. For example, Appreciative Advisors keep their arms uncrossed and lean slightly forward in their chairs because "You show respect and warmth by your open posture, your smile, and your vocal qualities" (Ivey & Ivey, 2007, p. 224). Attention to the details of nonverbal behavior will translate into quicker attainment of a comfort level that leads to advisee sharing of their stories, hopes, and dreams in the subsequent Appreciative Advising phases.

Advising Example

Trish [Receptionist]: Your 2 o'clock appointment has arrived and is waiting for you in the reception area.

Jenny [Advisor]: Thank you. I will be out there shortly to escort her back to my office.

[Jenny walks out to the reception area.]

Jenny: Hi Monica. My name is Jenny and I am glad you came in to see me [*shakes the student's hand*].

Monica [Student]: Hi.

Jenny: Please follow me back to my office [*escorts Monica back to office*]. Welcome to my office.

Did you watch the basketball game last evening, Monica? Wasn't that a great ending?

Monica: Yes—I actually got to go to it in person. The student section went wild after the game.

Jenny: I bet! I wish that I could have been there but I had to settle for watching it on T.V. Anyway, I'm glad that you are here and am hopeful that I'll be able to help you.

Monica: Me too. I am not sure what classes to take next semester. Can you help me?

Jenny: Absolutely, Monica—you have come to the right place.

Monica: Great!

Tool Box
Self-reflection

The first step to knowing others involves self-knowledge. Without proper self-reflection on one's own values, beliefs, interests, and preferred style, the advisor would find consideration of interaction strategies a difficult undertaking. As a means to enhance metacognition and self-development for professionals, self-reflection is highly promoted in professions involving teaching, interviewing, and counseling. We believe that advisors should practice self-reflection of their roles as advisors and enhance their self-knowledge.

The following is a list of questions to facilitate reflection on strengths and advising practice preferences (advisors should try to be as specific as possible in their self-exploration):

- What brought me into the advising field?

- When specifically have I felt especially fulfilled as an advisor?

- What aspects of advising do I enjoy the most?

- With what type of student am I most comfortable working? Why do I feel comfortable with this type of student?

- Among the traits that friends, peer advisors, or family members have identified as unique to my interaction style, which represent natural talents that make me a good advisor?

Generate Narratives about Advising

As a narrative-based approach, Appreciative Advising focuses on the value of story sharing and reconstructing. Before advisors listen to students' stories or narratives, they need to generate their own narratives to use in advising interactions to a) build trust and rapport with students via proper self-disclosure, b) invite students to make personal connections, and c) model storytelling that encourages students to share.

In generating one's own narrative, the Appreciative Advisor includes

- authenticity. No matter how moving and motivating the story is, if it does not reflect the storyteller's real experiences, it will be of little value in building a trusting environment. Authenticity is the most important feature of the Appreciative Advisor's narrative.

- asset-based stories. To model appreciative story sharing, the personal assets that advisors highlight in their own stories encourage students to take a strengths-based perspective when telling their stories.

- sincerity in storytelling. The purpose of sharing a story is not to teach a lesson or to preach a sermon. Appreciative Advisors want to develop a mutual learning situation where both parties gain from each other in exploring various paths to the student's success.

Summary

In summary, we conceptualized the Disarm phase as a means for Appreciative Advisors to make a positive first impression with students. Acknowledging students by greeting them with a full frontal stance (bodies turned squarely toward each other and direct eye contact) and warmly addressing them allow for immediate rapport establishment. In addition, an office decorated in inviting and self-disclosing ways encourages students to learn about advisors as caring helpers and may dispel some student anxiety. Appreciative Advisors also pay attention to nonverbal signals to maximize the chances of creating a long-term, meaningful relationship with students.

CHAPTER 5

THE DISCOVER PHASE

Discover: to see, get knowledge of, learn of, find, or find out; gain sight or knowledge of something previously unseen or unknown; to notice or realize; to identify (a person) as a potentially prominent performer.[2]

Discover

Perhaps Appreciative Advisors most enjoy the Discover phase because they learn from students during this period. Advisees arrive on campus with at least 18 years of experiences, dramas, and powerful lessons learned. They have earned awards and overcome hardships, some have saved lives, and all have impacted their families and friends. The Appreciative Advisor accesses these stories through questions. By utilizing positive, open-ended questions they can extract narratives through which they can help students identify their strengths, passions, and skills. In addition, the Appreciative Advisor becomes reenergized and reinspired by listening to students' stories.

Key Appreciative Advising Feature 5: Effective Open-Ended Questioning

The questions asked determine the types of answers received. Questions that do not invite elaboration (also known as "closed questions") typically beget yes-no answers. However, open-ended questions require the student to tell a story in their answer; thus, they provide powerful learning tools for the student and the advisor. "Stories illustrate causal relationships that people

[2]www.dictionary.com

hadn't recognized before and highlight unexpected, resourceful ways in which people have solved problems" (Heath & Heath, 2007, p. 206).

Furthermore, stories engage the imagination in ways that analytic discussions cannot. In the words of American author and storyteller Laura Simms (as cited in Watkins & Mohr, 2001, p. 77):

> Storytelling is acultural. As an art form, storytelling is not a solo performance of one person telling a story and someone else hearing their words. It is a very subtle transformative event that always takes place in the present and is reciprocal. Image is not something one speaks and the other hears. It is a very complex set of responses based on the listener's previous experience, openness, own well of imagery and association, and the speaker's own unspoken biases and capacities which comes from presence, intention, voice, understanding and openness to communication which is reciprocal.

Stories teach more about students than other methodologies. Therefore, Appreciative Advising strategies focus on the questions that will elicit stories from students. Sample Discover questions and statements used to solicit stories follow; several have been described by Wes Habley and Jennifer Bloom (2007) and all have been used successfully by Appreciative Advisors:

- Describe a peak experience when you felt really good about yourself or what you accomplished.

- Tell me a story about a time you positively impacted another person's life.

- Who are your two biggest role models? Why are they role models to you and what about them do you hope to emulate?

- Tell me about a time when you were faced with a challenge that you weren't sure you could overcome, but in the end you were able to do so. How did you overcome the challenge? What lessons did this experience teach you?

- Who had the biggest impact on your decision to come to this institution? How did they impact you?

- What were you doing the last time you lost track of time? When time just flew by and you looked up at the clock and thought it must be wrong?

These queries need not be asked in a specific order, nor should each student be asked all of the questions posted. Quite the opposite is true: Appreciative Advisors consider which avenues of investigation to pursue. The sample questions simply provide suggestions for launching conversations with students. The "insatiable curiosity" of the Appreciative Advisor mindset, not a predetermined question set, will serve the Appreciative Advisor best in the Discover stage.

In fact, Appreciative Advisors do not employ a checklist of specific questions. Instead, they ask broad questions, such as the ones listed above. Subsequent questions will vary by student because each one's story is unique. These follow-up tailored questions lead the student to reflect upon the positive experiences, strengths, and passions they possess.

In addition to the sample Discover questions listed above, we have also developed the *Appreciative Advising Inventory* (AAI)[3] to help advisors get to know students better, including their internal and external developmental resources. The AAI

---

[3]AAI development team members are Scott Amundsen, Jenny Bloom, Cathy Buyarski, Phil Christman, Amanda Cuevas, Linda Evans, Ye He, Bryant Hutson, Joe Murray, Claire Robinson, and Kaye Woodward.

is developed based on the premises of the 40 Developmental Assets developed by the Search Institute (2006)[4] and the literature on academic hope (Chang, 1998; Chemers, Hu, & Garcia, 2001; Snyder, Feldman, Shorey, & Rand, 2002; Snyder, Harris et al., 1991; Snyder, Shorey et al., 2002).

A copy of the AAI can be found in Appendix A. Advisors can use the AAI in a variety of ways to enhance the effectiveness of their advising sessions. For example, they can ask students to complete the AAI before the advising session and bring their results to the next appointment. Alternatively, they could request that students fill out the AAI during the advising meeting and debrief the responses as part of the session (ideally after the Disarm phase and after some initial rapport has been built via questioning). The AAI is available for free at:

www.appreciativeadvising.net.

Appendix B has a helpful chart that divides the inventory questions into subcategories reflecting the constructs of the questions and indicating whether the asset is internal (i.e., dependent on the student's beliefs and attitudes) or external (i.e., dependent on the student's environment or relationships). For each subcategory, we have provided a list of sample Discover questions that may be asked of students based on their answers to the AAI items.

Key Appreciative Advising Feature 6: Attending Behavior and Active Listening

Whether using Discover questions such as those illustrated above or questions based on assets uncovered through the AAI, advisors should demonstrate several important behaviors to make the most of the Discover phase. First, the advisor must listen carefully to each answer fully, allowing students to divulge

---

[4]The Developmental Assets® are used with permission by Search Institute.® Copyright © 1997, 2006 Search Institute, 615 First Avenue NE, Minneapolis, MN 55413; to learn more about Developmental Assets and to view the original framework, visit www.search-institute.org. All rights reserved.

their full stories, before drilling deeper by asking follow-up questions. The counseling literature describes the importance of the microskills hierarchy to counselors who want more effective communication with clients (Bobel, 2007; Ivey & Ivey, 2007). The infrastructure of the hierarchy is anchored on the advisor demonstrating four attending behaviors: the "3 V's + B":

- visual—eye contact,

- vocal qualities—tone and rate of speech,

- verbal tracking—sticking to the subject, and

- body language—authenticity (Bobel, 2007).

Each of these attending behaviors impacts the advising setting as much as counseling sessions. For example, making and maintaining eye contact throughout the appointment sends a clear message that the advisor is interested and involved in the student's story. Tone of voice should be monitored so that the advisor sounds inviting not condescending. Through verbal tracking, the advisor keeps the focus on the student, which discourages the conversation from going on tangents; a disorganized session dissuades the student from sharing more stories. Verbal tracking also helps to ensure that the student finishes her/his story before the advisor responds. Just as in the Disarm stage, the advisor needs to remember to lean slightly forward and sit with uncrossed arms.

As the student is telling his/her story, the Appreciative Advisor carefully observes the student. The exercise of such mindfulness, per the microskills hierarchy, is called "client observation skills" (Ivey & Ivey, 2007). The advisor is closely monitoring the student's verbal and nonverbal cues. Indicators that a student is truly passionate about something include the student talking louder, more quickly, and more definitively. The advisee may have a sparkling to the eyes and an excited voice. However, a student looking down and acting slightly annoyed is not interested in the topic at hand.

The advisor listens specifically for tales of the student's passions, strengths, and interests. She/he tries to find recurring themes throughout the conversation. For example, an Appreciative Advisor picks up on consistent stories about helping people from one advisee and those focused on complaints from another advisee. She/he is constantly taking mental notes about the student's accomplishments, strengths, skills, and passions. This information will come in handy during the Dream phase.

The advisor not only listens intently, but also participates in the conversation. Another layer of the microskills hierarchy is called "encouraging, paraphrasing, and summarization" (Ivey & Ivey, 2007). Encouraging behaviors include head nodding and affirming the student's statements. They encourage students to keep sharing their stories. Paraphrasing helps ensure the understanding of the student's statement, and when introduced with positive or complimentary phrases such as "I'm impressed by the fact that you...," it is particularly affirming. Similar to paraphrases, summaries are more in-depth descriptors of the student's narrative. When paraphrasing and summarizing, Appreciative Advisors point out specific times that the student took initiative and responsibility in situations.

Key Appreciative Advising Feature 7:
Strength-Based Story Reconstruction

The use of narrative storytelling in advising and interviewing is not new (Christman, 2005; Fiddler & Alicea, 1996; Hagen, 2007; Ivey & Ivey, 2007; Monk, Winslade, Crocket, & Epston, 1997). In narrative advising, advisors encourage students to reflect on their past experiences and tell their own stories. Through advisor questioning, the advisor and the student co-generate their past experiences and draw insights to guide action planning (Christman, 2005).

The narrative model used in counseling situations (Ivey & Ivey, 2007) depicts the basic steps of the strength-based storytelling process and can be applied to narrative advising in academic settings. Ivey and Ivey (2007) described the four-stage narrative model: story, positive asset, re-story, and action. In the first stage, students are encouraged to share their stories while the advisor actively listens. Based on the stories, the advisor facilitates the discovery of positive assets and strengths, and then the advisor develops the student's appreciation of his/her own stories. During the re-story stage, the advisor helps the student reconstruct the narrative by offering new perspectives of past experiences. The story reconstruction leads to the action plan.

In addition to promoting student storytelling and actively listening to students' narratives, advisors practicing the narrative advising model must monitor their own empathy during the process (Ivey & Ivey, 2007). The purposeful search and discovery of students' assets propel advisors forward, beyond the simple interchange of empathy between themselves and their advisees as they recast stories, to additive empathy, where advisors add new perspectives and facilitate a strength-based, prospective student view of their own stories.

Advising Example

Jenny: Before we start talking about classes for next semester, I first want to get to know you and your plans for your future. Can you tell me a story about a time that you positively impacted another person's life?

Monica: Hmmm. Let me think about that for a moment.

Jenny: Sure—take your time.

Monica: Well, I think the person that I have had the most impact on is my mom.

Jenny: How so?

Monica: Well, my mom is a single mother, and I have two younger siblings. My dad lives out of state and we don't see him very often. During my sophomore year in high school, my mom was diagnosed with breast cancer.

Jenny: I'm so sorry to hear that.

Monica: Thanks. It was quite a shock and it turned our worlds upside down. She initially had chemo, but that didn't kill the cancer, so she had to have a double-mastectomy. She was pretty sick for a long time, so I had to take care of my two younger brothers and make sure that they got to school, that their homework got done, and that they were fed. I also had to nurse my mom back to health.

Jenny: Wow! You really had a lot of responsibility taking care of both your mom and your younger brothers. How is your Mom now?

Monica: I'm glad to say that she is cancer-free and doing very well!

Jenny: That is great news. You realize that she couldn't have made it through her illness without you?

Monica: I don't know about that.

Jenny: I do. You really demonstrated great leadership and organizational skills at a very young age. You kept your family together and tended to their physical and emotional needs. On top of everything that was going on at home, how did this affect your academic performance at school?

Monica: It didn't have any effect. I just had to become more efficient in my studying, and my teachers were also very helpful and understanding.

Jenny: Well, that is an amazing accomplishment. I'm so glad that your mom is doing well. You obviously learned a lot going through that difficult time. I admire your resilience and persistence. Those characteristics will serve you well throughout your whole life.

Tool Box
Appreciative Advising Inventory **and Questions**

Advisors can use the AAI to understand the internal and external assets that advisees bring to college. The instrument has 44 questions divided into eight categories. The instrument was developed by a consortium of academic advisors from across the country. See Appendix A for the AAI and instructions about how to implement it. Appendix B features a list of questions that advisors can use when discussing a student's responses to the AAI.

Note-Taking Strategies

To reconstruct student narratives, advisors need to take mental or written notes to keep track of potential sources of motivation, assets that need to be highlighted or might have been overlooked, and resources that could be utilized. Table 5-1 is a template that can be used by advisors in taking mental or paper-and-pencil notes.

Whether taking mental or written notes, the advisor needs to facilitate storytelling through active listening and attending behaviors. Advisors preoccupied with writing down the conversation may inadvertently neglect the student, who may become more concerned about the content of the notes than self-reflection and story sharing. Therefore, we strongly encourage advisors to take mental notes or to explain up front the purpose in taking notes and inform the student that she/he will receive a copy of the notes at the end of the session.

Table 5-1. Guideline of Appreciative Advisor session notes (Discover)

Discovery Aspects	Questions to Consider	Comments
Sources of Motivation	What motivates the student in academic pursuits? The student wants to succeed academically mainly because...	
Assets Highlighted or Overlooked	In describing the student's academic success, he/she specifically mentioned... I noticed that the student has academic potential because...	
Resources	Based on what I know about the campus, the majors, and the student's interest, I think...	

Trombone Player Wanted

Using additional media resources can be useful at the Discover stage. Marcus Buckingham's *Trombone Player Wanted* (2007b) is a well-designed and informative set of six 12 to 14 minute DVDs that parallels his book *Go Put Your Strengths to Work* (2007a). While the formats can be purchased separately, together they work powerfully to describe the process of becoming individuals who put their strengths in their work and put their strengths to work. The DVD series is an exceptional resource for people who are interested in learning more about Buckingham's approach to strengths but lack the time to plow through the 270 pages of the book.

The DVDs are engaging. While they feature Buckingham sharing personal stories and interesting anecdotes, woven throughout the whole series is a compelling story about a young boy who dreams of being a drummer but is cast as the trombone player in his school band. As Buckingham provides his stories, the viewer sees images of the boy's development and his relationship with the band.

Short DVDs, such as those of Buckingham, can reinforce the usefulness and appropriateness of students identifying and discussing their strengths. They can be especially effective in classroom or group advising environments as a method to kick start a discussion. They can also be played in the advising waiting area to help set the tone for the upcoming advising session.

Trombone Player Wanted is just one example of media used to assist students through the Discover stage of Appreciative Advising. Dewitt Jones's DVDs (www.dewittjones.com), *Everyday Creativity*, *Celebrate What's Right with the World*, or *Focus Your Vision*, provide students, especially those with visual learning styles, other tools for exploring strengths.

Summary

In summary, the Discover phase is student focused. Appreciative Advisors use the power of positive, open-ended questions to elicit stories from students that capture their strengths, passions, and skills. They use appropriate attending and listening behaviors to encourage students to divulge their stories. The Discover phase is all about building rapport. Advisors who ask questions that elicit stories and are truly interested in student responses will find that they are able to engage successfully with their students.

CHAPTER 6

THE DREAM PHASE

Dream: An aspiration; goal; aim. A condition or achievement that is longed for.[5]

Dream

Hopes and dreams are precious possessions. In fact, they are so special that people do not readily share them. Some may fear that their dreams will be ridiculed or discouraged. Therefore, advisor rapport with students is crucial in the Disarm and Discover phases. Advisors need to establish trustworthiness so that students will reveal their wildest hopes and dreams for their lives. Perhaps many students answer the question, "What career do you want to pursue?" with a simple "I don't know" because they do not trust the questioner enough to share their true vision of their futures.

Key Appreciative Advising Feature 8: Creating Powerful Images

The Dream phase fundamentally differs from the Disarm and Discover phases, in which Appreciative Advisors focus on building rapport and encouraging students to recount past stories. "Dream activities bring a radical shift in energy and approach. More important, they stimulate creativity" (Whitney & Trosten-Bloom, 2003, p. 185). In the Dream phase of the model, Appreciative Advisors strive to understand the images in the students' minds. Creating a positive vision of the future is the first step in

---

[5]www.dictionary.com

accomplishing dreams. President John F. Kennedy, for example, planted an image in Americans' minds of a man landing on the moon by the end of the decade. Although many thought the dream unattainable, Americans inspired by the vision, not only saw that it was possible, they made it a reality.

Key Appreciative Advising Feature 9: Prospective Framework for Dreaming

President Kennedy's man on the moon seemed like the articulation of a nation's wildest dream, yet it transpired within the time frame envisioned. Likewise, articulation of the student's wildest hopes and dreams forms the first step to the future. Therefore, the setup to the Dream phase questions is critical. "I am going to ask you a question, but first I want to establish the ground rules. I want you to think big and not be restricted by the amount of education it takes, the probability of it happening, or other people in your life telling you it is impossible. Okay? Thinking big, what is your wildest dream for your future, including your future career?" Without building rapport in the Disarm and Discover phases and without encouraging students to dream big, advisors can expect an insincere answer, a response based on the student's perceptions of the advisor's expectations.

Here are some other Dream phase questions:

- Imagine that you are on the front cover of a magazine 20 years from now. The article details your latest and most impressive list of accomplishments. What is the magazine? Why have you been selected to appear on the cover? What accomplishments are highlighted in the article?

- When you were approximately 9 years old and someone asked you, "What do you want to be when you grow up?" What was your answer? What is your answer to that question now?

- Imagine that you are at our institution's graduation ceremony a few years from now. What do you hope your fondest memories of this place will be? What skills will you have then that will serve you well in your career and in your life?

- By the time you die, how is the world going to be a better place because you lived on this planet?

- Twenty years from now, what will your ideal work day be like?

At the beginning of this stage, the advisor and student can ignore practical issues about achieving dreams and the specific details of these dreams. The Dream stage motivates and helps students define success. Later, the advisor will ask the student to articulate the details of success and the steps for achieving it.

Key Appreciative Advising Feature 10: Making Purposeful Connections between the Dream and Discover Phases

The same attending and listening behaviors discussed in the Discover chapter will also serve advisors and students well in the Dream phase. Advisors continue to listen intently and purposefully because they are trying to make connections between the students' strengths and passions, as determined through their answers to Discover questions and their responses to the Dream questions. Are they congruent? Do their statements about their most cherished skills and abilities align with their stories about positively impacting other peoples' lives and their dream for the future?

Marcus Buckingham (2007a) pointed to a Gallup Poll survey that found that less than 2 out of 10 people feel that they are able to use their strengths a majority of time in their workplace. Buckingham defines strengths as "what makes you feel strong" instead of what other people think you do well. His definition of strengths is a powerful lens through which students can look, and advisors may want to invoke it when they find a disconnect or incongruence between the information about a student learned in the Discover stage and statements made in the Dream stage. If they want to help increase the number of graduates who can play to their strengths in the workplace, then Appreciative Advisors need to ask students, "What makes you feel strong?"

Advising Example

The following student scenario was initiated only after rapport had already been established with the student during the Disarm and Discover phases:

Jenny: I am really impressed by the fact that you have overcome so many obstacles before even stepping foot on this campus. You nursed your Mom back to health after she was diagnosed with breast cancer and you helped raise your two younger siblings while your Mom recovered. This is a lot of responsibility for a high school student to have and it sounds like you were not only able to help out at home, but you also were able to continue to earn good grades in school and be the leading scorer on the basketball team. If anyone has experience in balancing multiple demands it is you.

Monica: Thanks, I just did what anyone else would have done.

Jenny: Actually, not many people could have excelled in everything like you did. Now, let's start talking about your future. As you look into your imaginary crystal ball, what do you see as your wildest and most outrageous dream for your future?

Monica: Well, I know that I want to be happily married and have children—two to be exact. I also want to have a fulfilling career that allows me to help others.

Jenny: Tell me about this fulfilling career that you see in the crystal ball. What people are you going to help and how are you going to help them?

Monica: I know that I want to be a doctor who works with breast cancer patients. I don't want anyone else to go through what my Mom went through. But, I have always wanted to be a doctor. My parents bought me a Fisher-Price doctor's kit when I was 3 years old and I have known from that day forward that I want to be a physician. My mom has the cutest picture of me when I was 3 holding my doctor's kit.

Jenny: Excellent. By the way, I would love to see that picture. You will need to hang that in your office once you become a doctor. Keep in mind that there are two different types of medicine— allopathic medicine and osteopathic medicine. Allopathic medical physicians are known as M.D.s and it is the traditional route to becoming a doctor. However, there are also osteopathic physicians who are known as D.O.s. D.O. physicians are licensed physicians who are able to prescribe medicine and basically do everything that an M.D. does, but the osteopathic physicians have a slightly different philosophy: They take a holistic approach and tend to do more hands-on manipulating of the body as appropriate.

Monica: Is it more prestigious to be an M.D. or a D.O.?

Jenny: Good question. It is usually more difficult to get into an allopathic medical school, and there are more M.D.s than D.O.s. The important thing to keep in mind at this point is that there are two options. Another option would be to pursue a career in research. To do this, you would apply to graduate schools to earn a Ph.D. Yet another option that relates to working with breast cancer patients is a career as a physician's assistant, registered nurse, or social worker.

Monica: I'm pretty sure that I want to just be an M.D.

Jenny: That's fine, but I am just planting these seeds about the other possible options that you might have. You just don't want or need to cut off any of your options prematurely. I would encourage you to be open to learning about these other professions because if you become a physician your colleagues will be in those other professions.

Monica: Good point.

This scenario highlights the importance of discussing options with students from the beginning of the Dream phase. The Appreciate Advisor never discounts the student's idea about his/her own future, but they raise the student's awareness of other options and emphasize the validity in making alternate choices should circumstances or situations change (Jones, 1999).

Tool Box

Guided Imagining

Guided imagining facilitates student dreaming and imagination. It can be used to target the connections between a student's dream and current efforts to attain the dream.

Appreciative Advisors might encourage the student to dream and imagine based on the following script, improvising and adapting it as applies to the particular advising session and allowing the advisee to process the question. Advisors should remember to ask one or two questions at a time and to pause intermittently to allow the student to process or answer.

"I'd like you to close your eyes and relax."

"Imagine that you are getting up in the morning on a typical workday. You think about what you want to wear for the day. After examining your closet, what do you decide to wear? How are you feeling as you get ready for work? Excited? Anxious? What are you looking forward to at your working place?"

"Picture yourself eating breakfast before you go to work. Are you eating by yourself or with someone?"

"After breakfast, you step out of your door and glance around your house before leaving. What do you see? What are some things that mean something special to you at your house? As you look around your neighborhood, what do you notice? How are you feeling when you see your house and your neighborhood?"

"Now, imagine yourself heading off to work. How are you getting there? Is your workplace close? Far? What are a few things you notice as you drive to work?"

"When you get to your workplace, what is the first thing you see?"

"As you walk into your workplace, how do you feel?"

"Take a moment to look around your work space. What do you see? How many people are around you? Are you inside or outside?"

"What are you getting ready to do?"

"Now imagine the specific work you need to do today. What is the first thing you need to do?"

"Who do you need to talk with? How do you feel about the people you work with?"

"What is your day going to look like?"

"How about the day's activities that are ahead of you? Are they exciting, challenging, motivating?"

"What do you think is the significance of your job? Who do you impact? How do you make a difference?"

"When is it time for you to go to lunch? With whom do you go or do you prefer to have lunch by yourself? Where are you having your lunch?"

"It is now afternoon. How are you feeling about the activities you plan for the afternoon?"

"As your workday is coming to an end, how do you feel about yourself? What are some things you are especially satisfied or happy with?"

"What are you taking home with you?"

While doing this activity, the advisor must allow sufficient time for the student to dream and imagine. The advisor should practice pausing for 10 seconds; it can feel like a long time. Sufficient time for advisees to process after each question is critical to the success of this activity. The questions can be modified and effective in a group advising setting or as a class activity in a freshman seminar.

The T.V. Interview

The T.V. interview is a group activity. It is best conducted with 15 to 20 participants in a class or group advising session. The advisor should allow a full class period to complete the whole activity.

Students are asked to imagine being interviewed on an important talk show 20 years in the future. A real celebrity interviewer, such as Oprah Winfrey or Montel Williams, may be suggested as the host of the show. Students are asked to imagine how they would like to be introduced and the questions they would like to be asked. Students are then paired up to share their ideal introduction and the questions and topics they would discuss with the interviewer in that future interview. Through the pair and share, students are not only eliciting their own dreams of their future but also obtain various ideas from each other to widen their scope and perspectives.

In a variation, the advisor conducts the interview with the student in a typical one-on-one discussion. They would then debrief at the end of the session.

Four-Corner Index Cards

Advisors will find the four-corner index card a simple Dream activity that can be accommodated for either individual or group advising sessions. Advisors encourage students to explore their dreams using both writings and illustrations. Each student will be given an index card with four parts and be asked to:

- Write down three to five adjectives that your family, peers, friends, or others will use to describe you in 10 years.

- List the accomplishments that you will have already achieved in 10 years.

- Imagine that in 10 years a journalist interviews you and writes up an article about you. What would the journalist mention in the newspaper article?

- Draw a picture of yourself in 10 years. Be as specific as you can.

The index card would look like Figure 6-1.

Figure 6-1. Four-corner index card

A. Description	B. Achievements
C. Public Image	D. Self-portrait

Summary

In summary, the Dream phase elicits the hopes and dreams of the student. Appreciative Advisors help students create positive mental images of their futures. They also want to help students select careers that allow them to play to their strengths so that they can become part of the 20% who enjoys using their strengths a majority of time in the workplace.

CHAPTER 7

THE DESIGN PHASE

Design: To prepare the preliminary sketch or the plans for (a work to be executed). To have as a goal or purpose; intend.[6]

Design

Once the advisor understands the students' vision for their future, they can co-create a plan to make the dream come true. (Isn't it exciting to be in the dream-making business?) This plan will consist of concrete, incremental, and achievable goals. Marcia Baxter Magolda (2001) discussed the importance of students devising a self-authored plan, which is the heart of the Design phase. Notice that Baxter Magolda does not describe an "advisor-authored plan." The student authors the plan, and the advisor serves as an informed consultant to the student in this self-authorship.

Key Appreciative Advising Feature 11:
Teach Students How to Make Decisions

In the Design phase, the advisor acts as facilitator and guide. In one of their most important roles, Appreciative Advisors teach students how to make decisions. First, the Appreciative Advisor helps students brainstorm the options. Second, the Appreciative Advisor and student discuss the pros and cons of each option. Third, the Appreciative Advisor encourages students to thoroughly research their options and helps them determine the intended and possible unintended ramifications of each option.

---

[6]www.dictionary.com

Appreciative Advisors also discuss the importance of trusting oneself; that is, students should listen to their gut (especially if their gut is properly informed!). The bottom, nonnegotiable line is that the student needs to make the ultimate decisions. The advisor who decides for students does a disservice to those students. The students, not the advisor, must live with the consequences of the decisions.

To facilitate students' decision making, Appreciative Advisors might use a technique that Bryant uses with his students. For example, one of Bryant's undecided students is rapidly reaching the 60-hour mark and thus must select a major. She wants to major in either psychology or anthropology. After talking through the benefits and disadvantages of each option, the student is still undecided. Bryant grabs a coin out of his pocket and says, "Heads is psychology and tails is anthropology: You call it." Then he tosses the coin in the air. He catches the coin and puts his hand over it. Without revealing the coin, Bryant then says to the student, "Were you hoping it would be heads or tails?" and follows up with the question, "Why?" The student's answer to these two questions will reveal the deep-rooted choice that she was having difficulty putting into words.

Key Appreciative Advising Feature 12: Provide Positive Feedback

As an authoritative figure representing the university, the advisor who offers confirming feedback during the advising session can enhance students' self-confidence and self-esteem. Examples of this type of feedback include these phrases:

- "Excellent!"
- "You're right."
- "That's a good question."
- "Great idea!"

Only when students feel that their opinions are being heard and taken seriously will they genuinely engage in the Design phase.

Key Appreciative Advising Feature 13: Be Aware of the "Curse of Knowledge"

Appreciative Advisors need to use easy-to-understand language in advising sessions. Chip Heath and Dan Heath (2007) call this "being concrete." They define the "curse of knowledge" as the outcome when a very knowledgeable person fails to realize that others do not know the topic to the same level as she/he does. Appreciative Advisors avoid using confusing institution- or postsecondary-specific acronyms and jargon. Advisors must teach students to understand and maneuver effectively in the higher education culture, but those under the curse of knowledge may use language that reinforces a student's belief that the university is a complicated and inaccessible organization in which he/she has no place.

Jenny learned about confusing acronyms first-hand when she left the University of Illinois at Urbana-Champaign (UIUC) where she had spent almost 20 years of her career. Upon taking her new position at the University of South Carolina (USC), she quickly realized that the USC lingo, acronyms, and language were quite different than those at the UIUC. Jenny was constantly asking questions like, "What does GARP mean?" "What does SPA mean?" and so forth. Jenny has the experience and the self-confidence to ask clarifying questions. However, often for fear of looking stupid, students may not ask questions and become lost during the conversation.

The book *Made to Stick* (Heath & Heath, 2007) gives a great example of the potential disconnect between the message one assumes to be sending and the message the listener receives. In a graduate study, one person took on the role of "tapper" and the other played "listener." The tapper's job was to tap out a common song (e.g., "Happy Birthday to You") and the listener was to name the tune. The tapper had estimated that the listener would be able to guess the song 50% of the time. In the experiment, the listener guessed the correct song 1 time in 40. The tapper knew the song and was humming it in her head, so she thought the tune was clear. (Try this exercise with a friend. It really is difficult for the listener to know the name of the song without the context.) The same disconnect can happen between advisors and students when the former knows the context and is immersed in the culture but the latter does not; the advisor can easily overestimate students' understanding of the postsecondary culture.

Appreciative Advisors monitor the use of technical terms and acronyms. They also occasionally stop and ask the student, "I am covering a lot of material and sometimes I forget what it is like to not know some of the acronyms we use around here. Is there anything that I have discussed that you didn't understand?"

Key Appreciative Advising Feature 14: Making Effective Referrals

The plans created during the Design phase often involve referring students to external resources, such as other campus offices, alumni, people in the community, online resources, courses, and even other students. For example, in Jenny's former position as Associate Dean for Student Affairs of a medical school, her office maintained a database of graduates that was used to help current students network with alumni. Most of her medical students did clinical elective clerkships at other institutions. If one of these students wanted to apply for a clerkship in Boston, Jenny could print off a list, including contact information, of all the graduates that currently live and/or work in Boston. Likewise, if one of her students were interested in going into radiation oncology, she could print off a list, including contact information, of all the graduates that are radiation oncologists.

To make these referrals effective, the Appreciative Advisor not only points the student to the correct resource, but also clarifies the nature of the resource and the reason the student is being referred to it. For example, the advisor could specify to the student looking to work with an established radiation oncologist two or three of the radiation oncology graduates on the list of contacts. She would explain to the student why those alumni were selected. For example, they may have had similar career goals or similar research interests as the student. To make sure that the student is prepared to open up a discussion with the referred resource, the Appreciative Advisor and the student brainstorm on the best way for the student to make an introduction. The Appreciative Advisor should remind the student to mention the name of the person who had referred the student as well as discuss the kinds of questions that should be asked, how to take notes about important advice, and the follow-up thank you notes (or e-mails) to show appreciation.

Advising Example

The following is an example of an advisor walking the student through the Design phase of the Appreciative Advising model:

Jenny: Okay, we now know that your goal is to become a physician that treats breast cancer patients. In order to become a physician, you will obviously need to go to medical school. Keep in mind that once you graduate from medical school that you could do an oncology, radiation oncology, radiology, or surgery residency because all of these specialists work with breast cancer patients. The Association of American Medical Colleges has a great website [*Jenny writes down address for Monica: www. aamc.org*] that explains the medical school application process as well as the medical specialties I just mentioned. You certainly don't need to decide on a specialty today, but we should start to brainstorm together on some of the proactive things you can do right now to ensure you are accepted into the medical school of your choice.

Monica: Yes, that would be great.

Jenny: Well, to get us started, I'm going to suggest that you join the pre-med club on campus. I am going to give you this flyer that tells you how to sign up for the club and when their next meeting is. Joining this club is one clear way to show medical schools that you are truly interested in a career in medicine, and this group also does a lot of volunteer projects in the health care field. What other things could you be doing?

Monica: My roommate is pre-med and she said that it is important to be involved in a lot of activities to get into medical school. Is that correct?

Jenny: That is partially true. Medical schools are looking for candidates who are leaders, and one indicator of that is involvement in leadership activities as an undergraduate. For the most part, the quality of your experiences is more important than the quantity.

Monica: Should the activities all be health related?

Jenny: Certainly joining the pre-med club and eventually seeking a leadership position within that organization is a good idea, but medical schools want to see people who participate in activities that they really love. What activities are you already involved in?

Monica: My residence hall floor has a very active intramural soccer team, and I am the captain of the team.

Jenny: Great! What else?

Monica: I love to dance, and so I am on a hip-hop dance team that competes throughout the region. I absolutely love to dance, and this is a great stress reliever for me. It keeps me human, and it forces me to manage my time carefully.

Jenny: Excellent. As you have probably heard, there is a lot of information that you have to learn during medical school, so this experience with the dance team is teaching you time management skills, and you are learning how to balance your responsibilities.

Monica: That is for sure. I'm not exactly perfect at the balancing part, but I am getting better.

Jenny: Neither am I [*laugh*], but at least you are getting some experience grappling with this issue. Okay, anything else that you are involved in?

Monica: No, I think that is it.

Jenny: Okay, can you think of other things that you can be doing to help insure that you are a successful candidate to medical school?

Monica: Well, I did some volunteering at my local hospital back home when I was in high school.

Jenny: Great. Did you enjoy it?

Monica: Well, the first year I just delivered patients to procedures, but the second year I was able to spend a little time working in the emergency room and I absolutely loved that.

Jenny: What did you love about the emergency department?

Monica: I loved the fast pace and I was able to feel like I was helping more. I also got to see some really cool procedures.

Jenny: Your eyes really light up when you are talking about the emergency department. Why don't you go to our university hospital and see if you can get a volunteer position? You may not get into the emergency department right away. You may have to pay your dues working in another area at first, but it is appropriate to let the volunteer coordinator know about your experience and that you would ultimately like to work in the emergency department. However, you may also want to see if you can get some experience working with a physician in a different specialty so that you widen your exposure to the many different specialties within medicine.

Monica: That is a good idea.

Jenny: Keep in mind that your high school volunteering experience won't count when applying to medical school; the admissions committee is just going to focus on what you have done since you have been in college. So, in essence, you have a blank slate that you are trying to fill.

Monica: That is good to know. I didn't realize that my high school experiences wouldn't count.

Jenny: Don't get me wrong, your high school experiences were helpful in getting you into college and they helped reinforce your desire to become a doctor, so it wasn't like they were a waste of time. But it is a good idea to acquire experience working in a health care center as a college student. Here is the name and phone number of the volunteer coordinator at the university hospital [*printing off a sheet and handing it to student*]. Make sure that you tell her that I sent you to her. She is very nice but also very busy. Before you call her, you should look on the volunteer website that I have listed on the sheet with the phone number. Make sure you have your schedule in front of you when you go in to see her because she will likely want you to commit to a certain schedule each week.

Monica: Okay. I'll do that. Thanks for this info.

Jenny: What other things do you think medical schools are seeking in candidates?

Monica: I've heard that medical schools pay a lot of attention to grades and MCAT scores.

Jenny: Indeed, you need to be able to show medical schools that you can handle the rigor of medical school by having a strong GPA. In addition, you must pass a series of three licensing exams called the United States Medical Licensing Exams, or "USMLE," to become a licensed physician. So, performing well on the MCAT will demonstrate to schools that you have what it takes to pass the later USMLE exams, which are also standardized tests.

Monica: I have a 3.4 GPA so far. Is that good enough?

Jenny: I don't know. Is that good enough? Is that the best you can do?

Monica: Well, I should be getting straight A's, but I had a rough adjustment to college last year as a freshman.

Jenny: The good news is that medical schools know that the freshman year is where students usually have their worst grade performance. A 3.4 is strong, but from what I see from your high school performance and ACT scores, I would agree that there is no reason that you shouldn't be earning straight A's. What changes in your study habits would you need to make in order to make a 4.0 GPA a reality for you this semester?

Monica: I would probably need to spend less time going out with my friends. And, I know I should read before class, but usually I do not.

Jenny: Raising your GPA is going to be a matter of doing all the little things right. You hit on two of them; maybe just going out Friday and Saturday nights with your friends, but not on any week nights, might be a good start. Reading before class will also help you to make the most of attending lectures.

Tell me about the A that you received last semester in the honors section of Chemistry 101. That is not an easy class and not many people earn an A.

Monica: Well, I really enjoyed the professor's teaching style. There were a few times that I was stumped and I went in to meet with the professor during her office hours. She really helped me understand the concepts. Also, there was a group of us from the class that met three times a week in our dorm and we quizzed each other and helped each other out.

Jenny: Excellent. These are two proactive initiatives that you undertook that obviously had a positive impact on your grade in the class: You met with the professor during office hours and you formed a small study group. How about using these techniques in all of your courses this semester?

Monica: That is a good point. I can do that, although a couple of my professors are kind of intimidating.

Jenny: I know, sometimes they can be intimidating—even to me [*laugh*]. However, I have come to realize that professors are people too. They want you to be successful and the biggest complaint I hear from faculty is that no students come to see them during their office hours. One thing you might want to do before you go to meet with faculty members is to look up their websites. You will get a feel for the research they are conducting and when you go meet with them you can start off the session asking them about their research. Faculty LOVE to talk about their research projects.

Monica: Okay. I will do that.

Jenny: One last thing I want you to start thinking about now even though you are only a sophomore: letters of recommendation. I know it seems like a long way off between now and when you are going to be applying to medical school, but it really isn't that far away. You will be submitting your application the summer after this one.

Monica: Whoa! That is kind of scary.

Jenny: Yep. You are going to need 5 to 6 letters of recommendation to put into your credential file that the Career Center houses.

Monica: Who should I have write those letters?

Jenny: That is a good question. The general rule of thumb is that you want to have at least two from faculty members who taught science classes in which you performed well, one from a social science–type class, one from a supervisor where you volunteered, and another wildcard one. For example, if you decide to do undergraduate research, it would be a great opportunity for you to get a letter from the faculty member who supervises your work.

Monica: Okay.

Jenny: Keep in mind that I am not saying that you need to get all of these letters right now, but the important thing is to start building relationships with your professors like you did with your Chemistry 101 professor.

Monica: I guess that would also be a side benefit of meeting with my teachers this semester during their office hours.

Jenny: Absolutely.

Tool Box

Backward Designing

Backward design was introduced by Grant Wiggins and Jay McTighe (2001) as a method to facilitate curriculum design and planning. Through this method, teachers start at the end: They determine the student learning goals desired by the end of the unit and then they generate the questions that facilitate the student learning process (Wiggins & McTighe, 2001). Just like backward-design lesson planning, advisors also work with students in developing understanding that will lead to academic success. As Stephen Covey (1989, p. 98) pointed out: "To begin with the end in mind means to start with a clear understanding of your destination. It means to know where you're going so that you better understand where you are now so that the steps you take are always in the right direction."

Based on the model proposed by Wiggins and McTighe (2001), Appreciative Advisors identify the desired academic outcomes and use the following questions to inform practice:

- Based on the student's goals elicited from the Dream phase, what should the student be able to demonstrate after his/her graduation from college?

- What does the student want to see on her/his ideal resume?

- What does the student want to be able to tell any interviewer that he/she is capable of doing?

- What measures should be used to determine achievement of outcomes?

- How will the student's level of outcome achievement be evaluated?

- What indicators or evidence will show that the student has achieved her/his goal-based academic success?

- What academic experiences and learning activities would benefit the student?

- Where can the student find these beneficial experiences and activities?

- What resources are required for meeting goals?

- What are the learning behaviors needed to ensure academic success?

Keeping the end goal in mind, both the Appreciative Advisor and the student will be able to clearly identify the logical steps to achieve the goal. Such an advising session will also facilitate in the student a planning mindset for future academic pursuits.

In the advising example provided above, Jenny initiated the session by discussing Monica's long-term goal of becoming a physician and then focused the meeting on the means to utilize Monica's strengths to accomplish the short-term goal of entering medical school. In determining the means to measure for success, Jenny and Monica talked about the importance of leadership skills, experiences working in the field, and GPA and MCAT scores. For each of these measures, they collaboratively brainstormed ideas and actions Monica could take to increase her chances of being accepted into medical school. The final action plan for the student is not only applicable to the student's current position but also closely reflects the progress toward the student's long-term goal.

Graphic Organizers

Teachers frequently employ a graphic organizer to facilitate learners' concept building. It has been a proven way to facilitate the expression of ideas and their arrangement for visual thinkers. Graphic organizers are also known as "visual maps," "mind mapping," or "visual flow charts." Table 7-1 shows a graphic organizer applicable for Jenny and Monica in their Appreciative Advising session.

Table 7-1. Graphic representation of Appreciative Advising session: Jenny and Monica

| Long-term goal: become a physician |
| Short-term goal: go to medical school |

Requirement	Strengths	Action
Leadership skills	Team work and leadership experiences	Join the pre-med club and seek leadership opportunities in related area
Related experiences	Volunteer experiences at a local hospital	Seek volunteer opportunities at the university hospital
High GPA and MCAT scores	3.4 GPA Taking initiative to contact professor and start the study group in Chemistry 101	Read before class Spend less time with social activities Identify and take initiative
Good recommendations	Good experiences with the professor in Chemistry 101	Browse faculty website Contact faculty to discuss research interest

| Resources: Pre-med club flyer Volunteer coordinator contact information Career Center to sign up for Letter of Recommendation service |

Personal Presidential Cabinet

As the President and CEO of his/her own life, the student will want to make the best decisions based on the very best available information. Just as the President of the United States has a cabinet to advise her/him on any subject relating to the cabinet member's expertise, students need to surround themselves with people who are trustworthy and possess expertise in a wide variety of areas. As president, the student appoints and dismisses cabinet members at any time (Bloom, in press).

Appreciative advisors can apply the president and cabinet analogy and ask:

- Who is on your cabinet?

- Who are your role models?

- Who do you trust for advice on a variety of different topics?

Appreciative Advisors further explain that cabinet members serve as consultants and advisors but that the student should take the prized nuggets of information from each person and create the best solution for themselves. As when discussing the potentiality of possible futures, Appreciate Advisors should remind students that no single choice is definitive. As president, the student must live with the ramifications and consequences of the decisions, which means that he/she must be the sole and final decision maker. Students may need to be told that they can include fewer or more than nine cabinet members on their personal cabinet. See Figure 7-1.

Glossary List for Academic Advising

A glossary list created collaboratively by advisors in the office could serve as a tool to train new advisors and also let experienced advisors note the acronyms and technical terms that may be un-

Figure 7-1. Personal presidential cabinet

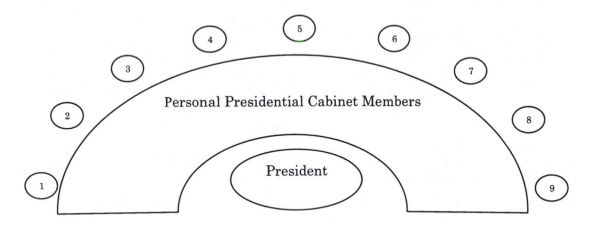

Who is on YOUR Personal Presidential Cabinet?

#	Cabinet Member's Name	I go to this person for advice on the following topics:
Example	Jane Smith	Career advice and ethical dilemmas
1		
2		
3		
4		
5		
6		
7		
8		

familiar for their student advisees. Table 7-2 provides a glossary list used by the Student Academic Services Office at UNCG.

Some advisees, especially transfer and international students, may benefit from a printout of such a glossary.

Table 7-2. Acronyms and jargon that may cause confusion for advisee, University of North Carolina at Greensboro

Acronym/Term	Definition
CAPP, pronounced "cap"	Acronym for the Banner "Curriculum, Advising, and Program Planning" module (online degree evaluation)
PGPA	At UNCG, the predicted GPA, a composite of the student's high school GPA and SAT scores, contributes heavily to the Admissions staff's decision for matriculation into UNCG
GPA	Grade point average
Academic Standing	A student's end-of-semester performance relative to the academic requirements for her/his classification
Academic Probation	A freshman will be placed on academic probation if her/his cumulative GPA falls below 1.75 A sophomore, junior, or senior will be placed on academic probation if his/her cumulative GPA falls below a 2.00 Any full-time, degree-seeking student who fails to pass at least 6 semester hours in a given semester shall be placed on academic probation
Academic Suspension	A freshman on academic probation will be suspended for one semester for failure to earn either a minimum 2.30 GPA each term or raise her/his cumulative GPA to 1.75 at the end of the probationary term A sophomore, junior, and senior on academic probation will be suspended for one semester by failing to earn either a minimum 2.30 GPA each term or raise his/her cumulative GPA to 2.00 at the end of the probationary term Students placed on academic suspension are denied permission to enroll for one semester
Academic Dismissal	A freshman who returns on academic probation after suspension will be dismissed for failure to earn either a minimum 2.30 GPA each term or raise her/his cumulative GPA to 1.75 A sophomore, junior, and senior who returns on academic probation after suspension will be dismissed for failure to earn either a minimum 2.30 GPA each term or raise his/her cumulative GPA to 2.00 Students who have been academically dismissed cannot enroll at UNCG

Table 7-2. Acronyms and jargon that may cause confusion for advisee, University of North Carolina at Greensboro (continued)

Acronym/Term	Definition
Academic Appeal	A student who wishes to appeal academic suspension and/or dismissal must appeal in writing to Student Academic Services by the appeals deadline in the academic calendar that is published in the *Undergraduate Bulletin* and semester *Schedule of Courses* Academic suspension appeals are considered in cases where circumstances beyond the student's control have interfered with the student's academic performance
Academic Recovery	Programming designed to assist students in improving their academic standing; SAS 100 is an example of an academic recovery program
GEC, pronounced "geck"	General Education Core
SI	Supplemental Instruction; if a student anticipates having trouble with a course, he/she is advised to take an SI course
SI	"Speaking intensive"; at UNCG, every student must complete two speaking-intensive classes for a degree
ESSI, pronounced "es-see"	The Early Spartan Success Initiative is the UNCG early warning system through which professors may submit information on students who are engaging in at-risk behaviors
Retroactive Grade Change	A student may submit an appeal to have grades retroactively changed to W. Appeals are only appropriate in situations that were "severe and out of the student's control"
Internal Transfer	Changing majors between schools (not departments within the same school)
Overload	A student can request permission to take credit hours over the 19-hour semester limit

Victim versus Creator language

For decades, psychologists have studied the impact of victim versus creator language on individuals' beliefs and behaviors. Jack Canfield, co-founder of the *Chicken Soup for the Soul* series, has probably done the most to introduce practical applications of the concept to the public. More recently, Kerry Patterson,

Joseph Grenny, Ron McMillan, and Al Switzler (2002) and Robert P. Crosby (1992, 1999) have described the significance of victim versus creator language in corporate organizations. David Emerald (2006) has discussed and expanded the concept in personal development and Skip Downing (2005) has provided applications of victim versus creator language in individual student success.

In this uncomplicated theory, language reflects personality. Creators are people who take full responsibility for their behaviors and beliefs and have an internal locus of control. Creators believe they compose their own lives and have choices. Victims, however, do not take full responsibility for their behaviors and beliefs; they see themselves as casualties of life. Victims have an external locus of control. Every day individuals choose to respond to situations as a creator or a victim (Downing, 2005; Emerald, 2006; Patterson et al., 2002).

Victim-Creator Road Maps

Victim versus creator language can be explained graphically in individual advising sessions or group advising programs. Although a number of models describe the victim versus creator languages, to move from being a victim to a creator requires a constructivist process; in other words, students will often describe multiple ways in which they have become creators when facing different challenges.

In one powerful application of the graphic organizer activity, the Appreciative Advisor asks students to describe a situation in which they had initially felt like a victim but then were able to become a creator. The students then map out the process on poster paper, describing the steps in which they had engaged as they moved from being a victim to being a creator. They can then describe challenges they are currently facing and apply their personal victim-creator road map to solving the new problem. Two examples of victim-creator road maps generated by students are shown in Figures 7-2 and 7-3.

Figure 7-2. Example of victim-creator road map

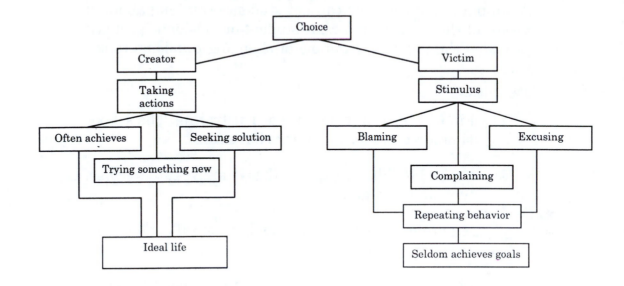

Figure 7-3. Example of victim-creator road map

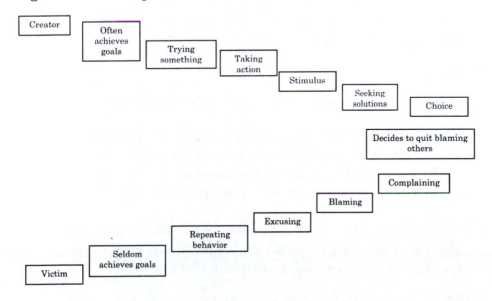

List and Respond

A simple list of concerns can get students thinking about the power of their chosen words. A student on academic probation provided the following example of changing problems to solutions:

Problems

1. Finding a parking space is so frustrating. The school shouldn't let noncommuters have cars.

2. I can't help the fact that I always arrive late to class. I have to work late.

3. My professor has it in for me. He just talks nonsense to the whole class.

4. I have to take way too many classes to meet general education requirements.

5. I have always had a difficult time with science. I feel like I can't pass the science requirements.

Solutions

1. I know I can find a space if I just come a little earlier.

2. [This is connected to item one.] If I get up when my alarm goes off then I can get to class on time or even early. So, I need to make arrangements to not work late when I know I have an early class the next day.

3. My professor is very knowledgeable about the subject. Maybe I just need to speak with him about why I am having a hard time understanding the material.

4. If I simply break it down to what I'll have to take each semester it won't seem as overwhelming. It will also be a smaller goal, which will be easier to accomplish.

5.   I need to go to tutoring to get some help with my
     biology [class] because it is not my strongest subject.

After the student made this list, the Appreciative Advisor followed up with a discussion of the student's assets and resources that can be leveraged to proactively handle current challenges. Students often have not taken time to articulate the roadblocks they face. When they take the time to think about their struggles, they can change the language they use to describe them. They use language to link strengths they currently possess to the problem, creating a powerful tool for articulating previous vaguely defined concerns and then turning them into a strength-based action plan.

Summary

In the Design phase, Appreciative Advisors and students co-create a plan to achieve the student's aspirations that had been uncovered during the Dream phase. Appreciative Advisors teach students how to make decisions and choices, provide positive feedback, and constantly monitor themselves to ensure that they are not speaking in jargon or with condescension. Effective referrals of students to campus, community, and other resources constitute an important part of the Design phase. Success in the Design phase manifests as student ownership of her/his own self-authored plan.

CHAPTER 8

THE DELIVER PHASE

Deliver: To produce or achieve what is desired or expected.[7]

Deliver

In the Deliver phase, the student executes the plan that was co-created in the Design phase. Although the student takes ultimate responsibility for carrying out the plan, the Appreciative Advisor increases the odds that the student will successfully deliver by energizing him/her with confidence in achieving the goals set forth in the Design phase. They also remind students that road-blocks will slow their attempts to complete their goals and they also teach them how to circumvent and/or overcome obstacles. Finally, the Appreciative Advisor follows up with students to check on their progress and remains ready to assist students who change direction as their plans evolve.

Key Appreciative Advising Feature 15: Energize Students to be Their Best

> Simply put, a leader's job is to energize others. Notice that I don't say it's part of their job; it is their job. There is no "time off" when a leader isn't responsible for energizing others. Every interaction a leader has is either going to positively energize those around them or negatively energize them. (Tichy, 2002, p. 297)

---

[7]www.dictionary.com

The advisor must take the initiative to sell the student on the necessary changes to complete the plan successfully. John Kotter (1999) stated that the first part of successfully implementing change is creating a sense of urgency. If a person does not understand the rationale behind the new initiative, she/he is less likely to follow through on it.

Jenny often speaks about the importance of students giving their best efforts so that they "won't wake up 20 years from now in a job that you hate because you did not make the most of the opportunities presented to you during college." Regret is a terrible burden to carry throughout life. Jenny often reminds students that many of their high school classmates did not have the opportunity to come to college and that it is a privilege and luxury to learn and grow on a college campus. She also quotes the four agreements, from Don Miguel Ruiz's (1997, p. 88) book by the same title:

- Be impeccable with your word.

- Don't take anything personally.

- Don't make assumptions.

- Always do your best.

While the advisor carries many roles, being motivator is perhaps the most important in Appreciative Advising. "Ordinary people believe only in the possible. Extraordinary people visualize not what is possible or probable, but rather what is impossible. And by visualizing the impossible, they begin to see it as possible" (Carter-Scott, 2006).

Key Appreciative Advising Feature 16: Engender Academic Hope

Academic hope (Chang, 1998; Chemers et al., 2001; Snyder, Feldman et al., 2002; Snyder, Harris et al., 1991; Snyder, Shorey et al., 2002) describes a powerful construct of positive thinking about academic abilities, setting goals, and realizing the ways to achieve those goals. If students think that only one road leads to their destination, they will likely give up when faced with a roadblock. Instead, in the Deliver phase, Appreciative Advisors must not fail to remind students that there really is "more than one right answer" (Jones, 1999).

Advising Example

Jenny: One last piece of advice: We have spoken about a number of proactive things that you can do to make your dream of becoming a doctor a reality. Just know that there are going to be roadblocks along the way. I don't want you to get discouraged if something doesn't go as expected. In fact, it's best to expect the unexpected. So, if you run into a problem, I want you to contact me right away because there is almost always more than one way to achieve a goal. Together we can discuss how to get around obstacles that you might encounter once you leave my office. Okay?

Monica: Yes, I will definitely get in touch with you if I run into any problems.

Key Appreciative Advising Feature 17: End the Conversation Well

Appreciative Advisors devote as much attention to the end of their conversations as the introduction. The last impression that the student has of the session will remain with him/her. Therefore, the Appreciative Advisor sends students off with a sense of confidence that they will be able to achieve the co-designed plan.

Appreciative Advisors review the plans and ensure that either students have written down the key points or have copies of the advisor notes. We prefer giving students a copy of our own notes so that we know the information they hold is accurate, but in either case, the student should leave with a written version of the next steps in the design plan.

The key goals of the Appreciative Advisor in ending the conversation include

- a review of the accomplishments made in the session,

- a reminder of the student's and advisor's responsibilities and the co-established deadlines,

- encouragement for the student to contact the advisor with any problems or concerns, and

- a reiteration of confidence in the student regarding the accomplishment of the goals set forth.

Appreciative Advisors say good-bye to students in a warm way. They escort the student to the door or the entrance to the main office and say something positive, such as "Thanks so much for coming in. I really enjoyed meeting with you. Please don't hesitate to contact me if you have any questions." Upon returning to the office, Appreciative Advisors ensure that any activities needed for or promised to the student get onto the to do list.

Advising Example

Jenny: Well, we have covered a lot of information today. I don't want to overwhelm you with info at this point, so why don't you make an appointment to come back to see me next month, after registration, and update me on your follow-through efforts on the plan we have discussed today.

Monica: Sure. I'll be happy to do that.

Jenny: Let's recap again what we've discussed today. I've written everything down here for you, but let's go over the list one by one.

Monica: That would be very helpful.

Jenny: First, you were going to join the pre-med club and contact the volunteer coordinator at the university hospital about opportunities there. Second, we discussed some concrete ways that you can reach that 4.0 GPA; you and I both know you have the academic skills and knowledge to earn it. Third, just like you did in your Chemistry 101 class last semester, you are going to start meeting with your professors on a regular basis and are going to try to set up small study groups. Fourth, you said you'd get to know your faculty members better so that you will have possible letter-of-reference writers down the line. Fifth, we talked about not going out on weekday nights, but still going out on Friday and Saturday nights.

Keep in mind that there is also free tutoring available at the Student Success Center—here is a pamphlet with their hours and the services they provide. Is there anything else I am missing? Do you have any questions for me?

Monica: No, I think that is a pretty good recap of what we discussed. Thanks so much for these suggestions. I feel really good about this semester.

Jenny: Me, too. I definitely think that 4.0 GPA is in your future! I am going to make a copy of my notes for you to help you remember what we have discussed today.

Monica: That would be nice.

Jenny: Great. Now is there anything else that we need to cover today?

Monica: No, I think I am all set for now.

Jenny: Super. I am really glad that you came into see me—this was fun. Sometimes the university can be an intimidating place, but I am here to help guide you through some of the land mines [*smile*]. I will look forward to meeting with you again next month. You can sign up for that appointment with the receptionist as I walk you out. Thanks for coming in.

Monica: Thank you.

Key Appreciative Advising Feature 18: Follow Up

Before the student returns for the next appointment, the Appreciative Advisor re-reads the session notes and the plan co-created at the last meeting with the student. The follow-up appointment is individualized and based on the previous appointment.

Even though Appreciative Advisors are often successful in building initial rapport with students in the first appointment, they will need to go through the Disarm phase when the student returns. In many ways, the Disarm phase at the second appointment seems easy because of the shared history together. The Appreciative Advisor prepares for the meetings such that the student will be impressed by the level of information the advisor remembers.

Objectives of the follow-up session include:

- reestablishing rapport quickly,

- getting the update on student progress since the last appointment,

- providing positive reinforcement as appropriate,

- assessing student progress toward goals.

- reminding the student that she/he can return when encountering roadblocks,

- reprioritizing goals based on the update from the student, and

- readdressing the Discover, Dream, and/or Design stage for student with changed goals.

Advising Example

Jenny: Monica, it is great to see you. Please come with me back to my office. I can't wait to hear about all that you have accomplished since our last meeting.

Monica: Hi! I can't wait to tell you about what has happened since our last meeting.

[*Jenny escorts Monica back to the office.*]

Jenny: So, first, tell me how your mom is doing.

Monica: She is doing well. Thanks for asking.

Jenny: All right, let's get to the good stuff: Tell me about all that you have accomplished since our last meeting.

Monica: Well, first, I have been doing really well in my classes. I was having trouble at the beginning of the semester with organic chemistry, but I have started attending tutoring sessions for it, and I have met with the professor a couple of times. I got an A– on my last exam!

Jenny: Excellent! You obviously are taking control of your academic destiny. Good plan to go talk to your professor and to get tutoring help! I am very proud of you!

Monica: Thanks. I signed up for the undergraduate research class and I actually spoke to my organic chemistry teacher about the possibility of working in his lab.

Jenny: Good for you. And what did he say?

Monica: He said that he wasn't sure if he was going to have an opening for a student next semester, but to follow up with him next month and ask him again about this because he should know for sure by then.

Jenny: That sounds promising. Of course, you don't want to put all of your eggs in one basket.

Monica: Exactly. That is why I also spoke to my biology teacher. I looked up her website and it turns out that she is doing prostate cancer research. Not exactly breast cancer research, but it does look exciting.

Jenny: The important thing at this point is to just get research experience. So, what did she say?

Monica: I have a meeting with her in her lab next week.

Jenny: Super. Make sure that you print off one or two of her articles that have been published recently and also look at the lab website before you go in.

Monica: Will do.

Jenny: Please be sure to let me know how the meeting goes.

Monica: I definitely will. I have also been checking out summer research programs and have found one that looks like fun.

Jenny: Remember that these summer research programs are competitive, so you will need to apply to 6 to 10 of them. Have you thought about who you are going to ask to write your letters of reference?

Monica: Yes. I think I will ask both my organic chemistry teacher and my biology teacher (the one that I am meeting with next week) to write me a letter.

Jenny: Both sound like good choices.

Tool Box

Follow Up

Appreciative Advisors use electronic calendars (e.g., Outlook) to paste reminders to follow up with students who do not return to appointments in the time interval established during the previous meeting. This proactive move clearly signals caring and a serious intention to help students accomplish their goals.

Questions to Close the Meeting with the Student

Examples of questions appropriate to ask at the end of a meeting include the following:

- Do you have any questions for me?

- Is there anything else that I should have asked you?

- In your mind, what is the muddiest point that we have covered today?

- Which of the things we discussed today are you looking most forward to doing?

- How and when will you keep me updated on your progress?

- What will you do if you run into roadblocks?

- What will you do if you think your goals may be changing?

Summary

In the Deliver phase, the student implements the plan that has been co-created with the Appreciative Advisor during the

Design phase. In the first part of the Deliver phase, Appreciative Advisors energize the student with confidence that he/she has the tools necessary to complete the plan. The Appreciate Advisor also reminds the student not to panic in the face of obstacles. The Appreciative Advisor intentionally ends the conversation with words of assurance that the student can indeed successfully carry out the plan. When the student comes back for a follow-up appointment, the Appreciative Advisor elicits an update from the student and then they work together to revise, modify, and prioritize the plan. Some revisiting of earlier phases may be warranted, especially if the student has decided to pursue other options.

CHAPTER 9

THE DON'T SETTLE PHASE

Don't Settle

Appreciative Advisors build rapport with their advisees for multiple reasons: Students who feel more comfortable sharing their hopes and dreams will be more likely to follow through on the plan that has been co-created with the advisor and will be more satisfied, as will the advisor, with the session. A strong rapport with students positions advisors to challenge students to be their best. Motivational speaker John Wright, Sr., reminded us that, "Our job as leaders is to help people become better than what they think they can become" (personal communication, December 12, 2006). Jim Collins (2001) asserted that few people attain great lives because "it is just so easy to settle for a good life."

The Appreciative Advising model does not espouse a touchy feely style of feel-good-for-no-good-reason approach; rather, it demands that advisors work hard to understand human behavior and to use both theory and the stories of students to prevent young promising adults from settling for a "good" life as they aspire toward a great life. Thus, the sixth stage of Appreciative Advising is called "Don't Settle."

Key Appreciative Advising Feature 19: Challenge and Support

Nevitt Sanford (1966, 1968) first expressed the concept that an appropriate balance must be struck between challenge and support such that students progress and grow. The balance is different for each student, which means that advising becomes an art form. We suggest that the words be reversed when referring to advisees: *support and challenge* better communicates the importance of establishing a trusting and supportive relationship that will be effective in subsequently challenging students. When the student knows that the advisor truly wants to help the student succeed, the advisor can expect more from students and encourage students to expect more from themselves.

Therefore, Vygotsky's (1978) ZPD theory plays an important role in the Don't Settle phase. The Appreciative Advisor recognizes that a student can achieve more with the guidance of a knowledgeable adult than she/he can achieve alone. The Appreciative Advisor carefully and artfully helps the student raise his/her own internal bar of expectations.

Key Appreciative Advising Feature 20: Raise the Bar

By simply being available to students, Appreciative Advisors start to lift the bar of expectations as the students grow in confidence. All of the previous Appreciative Advising stages have helped build and convey this confidence in the student. Laura Berman Fortgang (2007) observed, "Relationships are a key factor in your success, not because of what other people can do for you, but rather because of who you can become by being in their presence." Students indeed gain more self-confidence and empowerment than before meeting their Appreciative Advisors, but Appreciative Advisors get inspired by students and the progress they make toward fulfilling their goals. In addition, advisors who adopt the Appreciative Advising mindset become more effective and enabled professionals.

"The most basic way to make people care is to form an association between something they don't yet care about and something they do care about" (Heath & Heath, 2007, p. 173). Thus, the Appreciative Advisor is always drawing connections between student expectations and her/his hopes and dreams. As the bar goes up, the Appreciative Advisor clearly explains the reasons for its rise and aligns the student's previous accomplishments and strengths with his/her capability to meet this higher expectation.

In ideal situations, the student and advisor co-create the new standard for the student, but sometimes the Appreciative Advisor sees the student's unrealized potential and unilaterally challenges them to do better. B. Joseph White, President of the University of Illinois, explained, "I don't think that we're put into leadership jobs to maintain the status quo. I don't think we're put into leadership jobs to preside. I think we're put into leadership jobs to set high aspirations for the future and to achieve those aspirations" (Reiter, 2005, p. 22).

However, the Appreciative Advisor does not raise the bar so quickly that the student is in danger of being knocked over by it. If expectations are too high, the student loses confidence believing it cannot be readily achieved. Raising the bar to just the right level at precisely the right time takes an artist who understands her/his subject: It takes an Appreciative Advisor who understands general human behavior and who knows the stories and dreams of the advisee.

Key Appreciative Advising Feature 21:
Virtuous Cycle

Meeting with a student multiple times allows Appreciative Advisors the opportunity to highlight the important strengths that students demonstrate and their successes they accumulate based on accomplishments made during the Deliver phase. This momentous energy powerfully establishes a virtuous cycle.

In "a virtuous cycle, an improvement in one area leads to an improvement in another area, which then leads to further improvement" in the original area, and so on (Orem, Binkert, & Clancy, 2007, p. 53). Advisors are instrumental in guiding and reminding students to create and maintain positive self-reinforcing cycles of thought, emotion, and actions.

The virtuous cycle is the exact opposite of a downward or vicious cycle, where the student becomes so consumed by self-doubt and emotion that the negative chain of events is difficult to break. The virtuous cycle is just as difficult to break as the vicious cycle because the positive reinforcement continues, providing the student with a high level of resilience to deal with unforeseen roadblocks.

Advising Example

Jenny: Monica, earlier you mentioned getting an A– on your latest organic chemistry test, which is great. How are the rest of your classes going?

Monica: Pretty well.

Jenny: Okay, run me through them one by one, letting me know what your grade is in each class.

Monica: Well, with the A– on the latest organic chemistry class, I think that brings me up to a B or a B+. I'm also taking an English literature course, and I think I have somewhere between a B and an A– going in that class. Then I'm also taking calculus, and I didn't do so well on my last test, so my grade went from an A to a B+.

Jenny: So, it sounds to me like you are in the B+/A– range in all of your classes?

Monica: Yes, I would say that is pretty accurate.

Jenny: First, there is absolutely nothing wrong with B+/A– grades. Many people would be thrilled to earn those grades. However, if I recall correctly from our last meeting, your goal is to have a 4.0 GPA this semester. What things have you done right this semester toward achieving that goal?

Monica: Well, like I mentioned earlier, I have been going in to see my organic teacher.

Jenny: Great and doing so paid off in earning an A– on your last test. So, have you been in to see your other teachers?

Monica: I've been meaning to, but I just haven't gotten around to it.

Jenny: Well, there is no time like the present. Who do you have for calculus and for English literature?

Monica: Dr. Jones for calculus and Dr. Smith for lit.

Jenny: Okay, I happen to know both of these folks and they are very nice.

Monica: You are right. I'll make an appointment to see them both when I get home today.

Jenny: Great. What else should you be doing?

Monica: Well, I have still been going out on Thursday nights in addition to Friday and Saturday nights. I guess I need to buckle down and spend Thursdays studying.

Jenny: Makes sense to me. Monica, the bottom line is that I know that you have the intellectual firepower to get straight A's. I just don't want you to look back and regret not taking advantage of the opportunity to push yourself and to accomplish your goals. The number of applications to medical school keeps rising, so you need to put yourself in a position that your GPA is as high as it can possibly be because we don't know how high the GPA bar will be set by the time you are applying to medical school.

Monica: You are absolutely right. I need to get my butt in gear and start performing in classes like I know I am capable of doing.

Jenny: And let me make it clear that I see your potential and want to do everything I can to help ensure that you are a successful doctor. As humans we have this tendency to settle for good enough and I want to encourage you to keep raising your own internal bar of expectations. For example, although you feel like you are overwhelmed right now with your classes, activities, and stuff, keep in mind that when you enroll in medical school you will be taking a full load of 9 to 10 science classes and will in essence be in classes all day long. The more you can challenge yourself right now and learn the basics from your science classes the more it will pay off for you when you go to medical school.

So, given all that I have said, what more can you be doing to prepare yourself to become a physician?

Tool Box

Appreciative Advising Rubric and Evaluation

Ongoing self-assessment is a necessary component in effectively conducting Appreciative Advising and developing over time as an advisor. Table 9-1 illustrates an Appreciative Advising rubric and evaluation tool for advisors to use to monitor their own growth.

Personal Success Letters

Personal success letters can be a great capstone assignment for a first-year experience or an academic recovery course, but a student may do it as a follow-up to an advising session. In this activity, the student writes an anonymous letter to be given to a student in the same circumstances as the writer in the following semester. For example if the student is currently on academic probation, the letter would be written to a student who is placed on academic probation the next semester. The letter might include a simple self-introduction, a description of self-knowledge acquired during the probation semester, advice for a student who has been recently placed on probation, and reflections on the recovery program. If the activity is part of a first-year experience course, the letter might emphasize the student's advice for achieving success during the first year of college.

Table 9-1. Appreciative Advising rubric and evaluation

Appreciative Advising Stages and Features	Evaluation		
Disarm	**Good**	**Better**	**Best**
1: Warm Welcome 2: Safe and Comfortable Environment 3: Appropriate Self-disclosure 4: Appropriate Nonverbal Behavior	Advisor focuses only on the content of advising; considers advising as facilitating course registration. Student does not feel engaged or connected.	Advisor focuses on both content and the student in advising. Student provides some input in the discussion.	Advisor makes personal connections with the student in advising; considers advising as student-centered. Student feels engaged and makes personal connections with the advisor.
Discover			
5: Effective Open-Ended Questioning 6: Attending Behavior and Active Listening 7: Strength-Based Story Reconstruction	Advisor asks strength-based questions. Student reflects on past experiences.	Advisor asks strength-based questions based on student stories. Student reflects on assets.	Advisor not only asks questions, but also reconstructs the stories to highlight student assets. Student tells and listens to their stories with their assets highlighted.
Dream			
8: Creating Powerful Images 9: Prospective Framework for Dreaming 10: Making Purposeful Connections between the Dream and Discover Phases	Advisor asks about student's future plan. Student is encouraged to think about the future.	Advisor encourages student to dream of the future. Student creates future images in day dreams.	Advisor facilitates student dreaming based on the assets discovered. Student constructs future image based on strengths and assets.
Design			
11: Teach Students How to Make Decisions 12: Provide Positive Feedback 13: Be Aware of the Curse of Knowledge 14: Making Effective Referrals	Advisor constructs academic plan for the student. Student is informed.	Advisor constructs academic plan based on student input. Student is informed and her/his comments and input are valued.	Advisor facilitates student constructing his/her own academic plan and provides input and feedback. Student is the designer of the plan and advisor's input is valued.
Deliver			
15: Energize Students to be their Best 16: Engender Academic Hope 17: End the Conversation Well 18: Follow up	Advisor completes the session with the student and considers it the end of advising. Student is left alone to follow the plan and strive for academic success.	Advisor encourages the student to follow up and keep advisor informed of her/his academic life. Student knows that they can seek advisor to address further questions.	Advisor designs plan for follow-up before conversation ends and follows up with the student in a consistent manner. Student is monitored and facilitated between advising sessions.
Don't Settle			
19: Challenge and Support 20: Raise the Bar 21: Virtuous Cycle	As long as the designed plan has been followed, both the advisor and the student are satisfied.	Advisor encourages student to set higher expectations after initial success.	Advisor has high expectations for the student and purposefully provides challenge and support to encourage student to have high self-expectations.

This letter achieves several goals that are appropriate for the Don't Settle phase. First, it gives the advisor insight into how an advisee is thinking about his/her own achievements and self-expectations, legacy as a student, and gains from participating in the Appreciative Advising process.

Students need to experience success before they are challenged, and this activity requires that they reflect upon their recent successes. Furthermore, students need to establish virtuous cycles where they continuously build on past successes; with this letter they recognize that their achievements for the semester have been so significant that others may build upon them.

Second, it allows the advisee a concrete way to leave a legacy. The Don't Settle phase is about self-monitoring and self-challenging to promote personal growth. The letter emphasizes that the student makes a difference and has influence on her/his peers. Additionally, writing the letter requires reflection on how personal experience is valuable to oneself and to others.

Third, the student who receives the letter is given a sense that he/she is not facing the academic experience alone, but that others in similar circumstances have already successfully negotiated this roadblock. Students sense that others on campus have similar experiences and are supporting them.

Simple Truths Web Slide Show Series

The free web slide show, "212: The Extra Degree," is available at www.212amovie.com, distributed by Simple Truths, LLC, and is based on the book by the same name. It shows the profound difference a little bit of extra effort can make in life and business. A short 3-minute presentation, the central points are as follow:

- Perseverance is not one long race: It is a series of short ones.

- Small differences can make a life-changing impact.

- One small move can make the difference between being good and being great.

- To achieve your goals, you must be willing to do things you've never done before.

- It's your life. You are responsible for your results.

"The Dash: Making a Difference in Your Life" is another Simple Truths web slide show available on the Internet at www.thedashmovie.com. Based on a poem that has been circulating for some years, it emphasizes the importance of living an Appreciative, mindful life. The two presentations when taken together capture many of the themes of the Don't Settle stage.

Summary

The rapport that has been established in the earlier phases is the springboard to effectively challenge students to reach their true potential. Advisors do this by helping students raise their own internal bar in terms of their self-expectations. Each student is unique and thus the level and timing of challenges to students vary. To believe that they can accomplish the larger goals, students need to experience success before they are challenged. The ultimate Appreciative Advising goal remains: Students need to establish virtuous cycles where they continuously build on past successes.

Section III:

Applications

CHAPTER 10

OVERVIEW OF PROGRAMMATIC INITIATIVES

In addition to individual and group advising sessions, Appreciative Advising applies to programs designed for special purposes or populations. In this section, we discuss the application of Appreciative Advising to advising programs at UNCG for students on academic probation, first-year college students, internal-transfer pre-nursing majors, and students who are readmitted after dismissal. A discussion of effective program development and administration to integrate Appreciative Advising follows (Chapter 11). Finally, the general evaluation design for Appreciative Advising–integrated programs allows for tracking the effectiveness of programs (Chapter 12).

Strategies for Academic Success 100 Course

Program Description

At UNCG, any freshman who earns a cumulative GPA below a 1.75 and any sophomore, junior, or senior whose cumulative GPA falls below 2.00 is considered on academic probation for the next semester. These students on probation must attend the Strategies for Academic Success (SAS) 100 program, which is an 8-week, pass/fail, noncredit course that combines mandatory classroom attendance with regular face-to-face meetings with the instructor.

The SAS 100 program, introduced in the 1999-2000 academic year as a full-semester course by the UNCG Student Academic Services office, featured a remedial study-skills curriculum. Since then, several modifications, based on program evaluation results, have translated into better meeting the needs of students. The full-semester course was revised to an 8-week curriculum so that students can benefit from the course content before the midpoint of the semester. Furthermore, mandatory individual student conferences ensure ongoing communication between the instructor and the student. Appreciative Advising was infused into the program to guide the individual student conferences and to facilitate students' exploration of their personal and academic strengths as a means of devising an academic-recovery plan. The program goals are as follow:

1. to facilitate the development of student academic strategies,

2. to encourage students to self-reflect on their academic strengths, and

3. to provide support for students to achieve academic recovery.

Actively reflecting on past successes and personal strengths, the students in the SAS 100 program learn to act interdependently and gain personal insights by taking responsibility for their actions, managing their behaviors, and believing in themselves. They then set goals accordingly. The program design is geared to help students on academic probation meet the academic good-standing policy standards for the institution.

The Appreciative Advising theoretical framework works for the SAS 100 program for several reasons. Selective institutions such as UNCG have identified enrolled students as being capable of success and completing their degrees, and thus it has already invested resources in these students. Therefore, assistance rendered from a deficit-based paradigm (i.e., looking for areas of academic weakness or poor time management) seems counterintuitive to a university that matriculates students who have already shown academic success. In addition, students with poor academic standing typically have a very limited time in which to recover. Building on strengths, and engaging in academic and social behaviors that reflect these strengths, is a more efficient strategy than attempts to correct long-standing deficits (Gouker et al., 2008; Hutson et al., 2005).

Key Features of SAS 100

Mandatory Participation. The course starts at the beginning of the second week of classes so that all students have an opportunity to enroll in it. Students required to take SAS 100 and who fail to register for the class are immediately suspended. This extreme consequence forces students to take the course seriously, which is essential to its effectiveness (Kamphoff et al., 2007). Students are also suspended if they miss a class meeting. However, students can appeal the suspension.

Group Interaction among Students. In addition to the emphasis on Appreciative Advising, the SAS 100 program promotes interaction among students. The students interact in a small group setting where reflection and self-disclosure occur regularly. Each student is encouraged and guided to discuss her/his experiences while other students provide support. In this way, a nurturing environment is generated for students to relate to others in academic jeopardy (Kamphoff et al., 2007).

Individual Meetings with Instructors. Furthermore, each student is required to meet with the assigned SAS 100 instructor twice during the 8 weeks of the course. In these meetings, the instructor asks intentionally positive questions (e.g., "When was the last time you felt most alive in the classroom?") that require students to tell narrative stories of past academic successes. This type of discussion reinforces past accomplishments and allows the student to relive these positive experiences (Hutson et al., 2005).

Appreciative Advising Inventory.[8] Students take the AAI (Appendix A) as an online instrument and have the results sent to the advisor before the first appointment. The advisors

---

[8]The Developmental Assets® are used with permission by Search Institute.® Copyright © 1997, 2006 Search Institute, 615 First Avenue NE, Minneapolis, MN 55413; to learn more about Developmental Assets and to view the original framework, visit www.search-institute.org. All rights reserved.

use the results of the instrument to start the conversation with the student and build the student strength profile through the discussion.

Results

Ongoing evaluation of the program not only facilitated the improvement of the program, but also illustrated its effectiveness. After the implementation of the SAS 100 courses, the retention rate of students on academic probation was higher in all years subsequent to its introduction, showing from a 9% increase the second year to as much as an 18% increase for the two consecutive academic years (2002-2004) after Appreciative Advising was introduced. See Figure 10-1. In addition, when control and treatment groups were compared in terms of their GPA gains over one semester, the treatment group demonstrated statistically significant higher GPA gains than the control group ($p = .03$) (Kamphoff et al., 2007).

Beginning in spring 2002 and continuing through spring 2005, SAS 100 students responded before and after taking the course to the *Student Strategies for Success Survey* (Hutson, 2003). Used to measure changes in academic self-efficacy, the instrument has six subscales: Academic Preparedness, Confidence, Dedication, Interdependence, Self-Knowledge, and Social Behavior. Results showed statistically significant positive changes in four of the six subscales, indicating that the students had adopted positive behaviors and were enjoying more success in their academic and personal lives. See Table 10-1. This information was cross-validated through face-to-face interviews that were also conducted with students prior to and after attending the course. A high level of congruence was identified between student survey and interview results (Hutson, 2006). Similarly, when longitudinal data from several semesters were examined, a trend toward overall effectiveness in the program was observed (Kamphoff et al., 2007).

Figure 10-1. Percentages of students on probation retained after completion of SAS 100

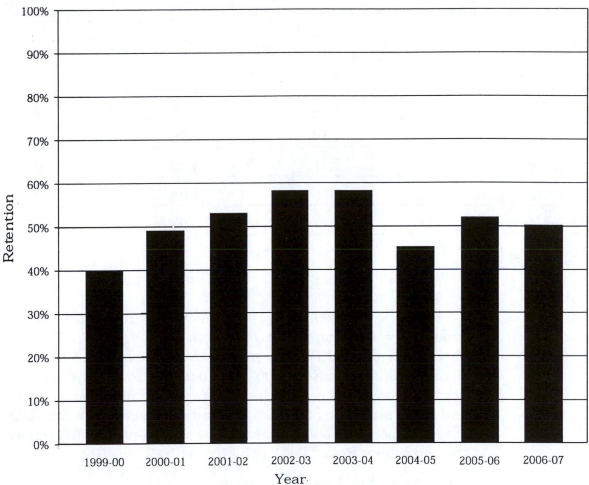

Table 10-1. Changes in academic self-efficacy of SAS 100 students, per *Student Strategies for Success Survey*, combined data 2002–2005

Subscales	Pretest		Posttest		t
	$\bar{X}$	SD	$\bar{X}$	SD	
Academic Preparedness	3.50	1.75	3.71	.61	1.65
Confidence	4.22	.53	4.38	.46	3.26*
Dedication	4.16	.78	4.26	.73	1.34
Interdependence	3.21	.75	3.42	.72	3.07*
Self-knowledge	3.56	.70	3.98	.60	6.97*
Social Behavior	3.77	.67	4.05	.57	4.67*

Note. *$\alpha \leq .008$.

During spring 2003, SAS 100 students ($n = 203$) and a control group ($n = 119$) completed *The Adult Trait Hope Scale* by C. Richard Snyder and *The Revised Life Orientation Test* by Michael Scheier (as cited in Rolo, 2004). Students were surveyed at the beginning of the semester, the end of the SAS program, and the end of the semester. Statistically significant changes in SAS 100 students' hope and optimism scores were evident ($p < .01$) across the semesters (Rolo, 2004). See Figures 10-2 and 10-3.

University Studies 101 Course

Program Description

Based on perspectives emerging from Appreciative Advising, the University Studies (UNS) course was developed at UNCG for first-semester college students. Two sections are offered: UNS 101 for new freshmen and UNS 102 for new transfers. Although full-semester graded courses, UNS classes are not required and count as a one-credit elective toward the degree. The Student Academic Services Office at the university, which administers the

Figure 10-2. Academic hope development

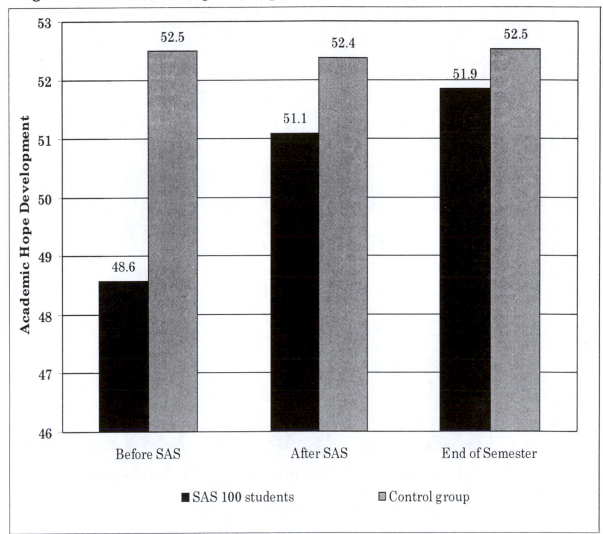

UNS program, provides information about the class at orientation sessions for entering students (Hutson & Atwood, 2006).

University staff and faculty volunteers teach UNS 101. The textbook, written by university staff and faculty, is updated and printed annually to reflect changes in the curriculum and in institutional policies and programs. Providing the core of the curriculum, the text deals with making the transition to

Figure 10-3. Academic optimism development

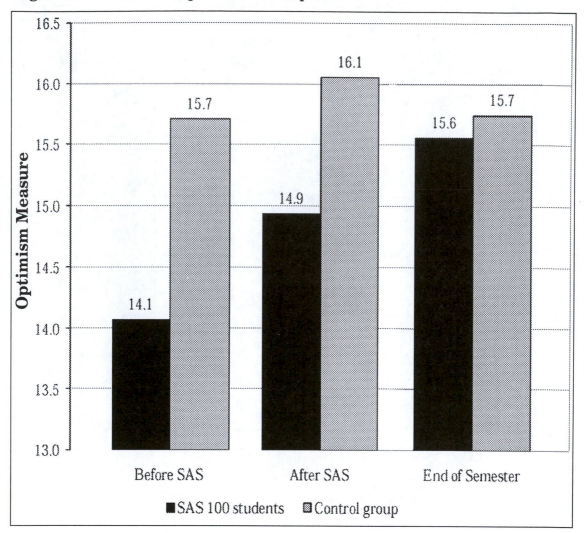

the institution, academic and campus resources, motivation and goal setting, time management, the institution's history, learning styles, note taking, study and test-taking skills, library resources, academic advising, career planning, maintaining a healthy lifestyle, multicultural concerns, leadership and civic engagement, and money management. While the curriculum focuses on academic and life skills, class activities include field trips to pertinent campus resources, an off-campus ropes-course activity, and in-class interactions with a number of campus representatives (Hutson & Atwood, 2006).

Key Features of UNS 101

Peer Academic Leaders. A unique feature of the UNS 101 program, Peer Academic Leaders (PALs) are primarily juniors and seniors who have achieved academic success and who serve as role models for new students and mentor them for success. A PAL is assigned to each class to help promote community and campus involvement as well as to facilitate events and activities.

Strengths-Purposes-Aligning. The UNS program emphasizes the Appreciative Advising theoretical framework for several reasons. The stated aim of the program is to assist students in identifying their *strengths*, discovering their *purposes*, and *aligning* these newly discovered assets with a plan for their future. The activities, class discussions, and assignments guide students through the stages of identifying strengths, discovering purposes, and finding alignment. Some UNS instructors have started to use an acronym, "SPA," to describe this process.

Additional sections of the course address the specific needs of nontraditional and international students; however, these students need not choose these sections to participate in the class. The instructors for these sections work with these populations specifically in their other functions at the university.

UNCG students are highly diverse in terms of cultural background, ethnicity, as well as socioeconomic background, and enrollment in the UNS program reflects the demographics of the campus. Appreciative Advising can be powerful in that, through the questions advisors ask, students are empowered to establish the set of values, concerns, and goals of the dialogue. Rather than establish acceptable strengths and purposes, the instructor encourages UNS students to explore their personal strengths and purposes without concern about whether the instructor approves of the students' personal and/or cultural values. Through grading rubrics and written feedback, the instructor reacts to students' self-exploration through probing questions and setting standards for quality self-expression (Davis, Funderburk, & Hutson, 2008).

Results

In fall 2007, Student Academic Services offered 45 sections of UNS 101 with 1,023 students enrolled. It offered three sections of UNS 102 with 46 students enrolled.

Because evaluating the program quality and its impact on students is a high priority, each class is carefully monitored to ensure that the curriculum and activities are standardized across instructors. The program has been constantly evaluated since its implementation in the fall of 1998, and the program and its curriculum have been modified as more is learned about student needs and the impact of the program on student persistence and academic outcomes.

UNS students have consistently indicated development in their levels of academic preparedness and confidence as well as their ability to develop and maintain interdependent relationships with faculty members, university staff, and peers. They also describe an improved understanding of themselves as individuals, improved academic self-efficacy, and a greater sense of major and career goals (Hutson & Atwood, 2006).

Evaluation results provide evidence that students who take a UNS course consistently have higher cumulative GPAs and are more likely to remain enrolled and graduate from the university than those who do not take it. The retention rate of freshmen who completed UNS 101 in fall 2006 and returned for fall 2007 was 81.9%; of those who did not take the course, 74.4% were retained over the same period (Davis et al., 2008).

UNS 101 was ranked 8th out of 51 peer institutions in course effectiveness in 2005 by the *First-Year Initiative Survey* of the Policy Center on the First-Year of College. This ranking is determined from surveys completed by students in orientation courses in participating institutions.

Internal Transfer Program for Pre-Nursing Majors

Program Description

Appreciative Advisors ask questions that trigger a student's exploration of passions and strengths to promote an improved academic experience. This approach is particularly useful for students whose declared major may not be a good fit and who may be struggling to identify a new one. Since spring 2005, Appreciative Advising has been used at the UNCG with pre-nursing majors who have not met the Nursing program's rigorous academic standards required for admission into the major. By helping students devise strengths-based academic recovery plans that align students' strengths with new potential majors, Appreciative Advisors have helped a number of these advisees feel empowered as students. They have also assisted these students in identifying new majors and earning greater academic success in terms of higher GPA and progress toward degree (Atwood & Hutson, 2006).

At UNCG, pre-Nursing majors must earn a cumulative 2.00 GPA to remain a declared major after their first semester, and after completing 30 semester hours they must maintain a 2.70 GPA. Nursing majors who do not meet these requirements must consider an internal transfer to a new major.

In the intervention a Student Academic Services advisor, who is trained in Appreciative Advising, takes over duties from the nursing faculty member who had advised the student. The new advisor works through the stages of Appreciative Advising with the student, focusing on helping him/her align strengths with an alternative major. This advising program involves three meetings during the first semester of advising. The first meeting lasts an hour during which time the advisor and student discuss the strengths of the student, the student's stories about becoming a pre-nursing major at UNCG, and the idea of another major. Students complete two worksheets, developed from the Appreciative Advising model, in which they answer questions about when they feel successful overall and about their academic strengths.

Students also take the online AAI instrument like participants in the SAS 100 program do. The results are sent to the advisor between their first and second appointments. In the second appointment, they discuss the AAI results, alternative majors, and registration for the next semester. The final session includes a discussion of the final schedule and change of major.

Results

The initiative is being evaluated through comparison of change-of-major rates, cumulative and semester GPAs, and graduation rates of nursing students who had the benefit of the internal transfer program and those who were forced to transfer before inception of the program. Longitudinal data about participants' retention rates, GPAs, and major changes were collected and analyzed. See Table 10-2. Participants are surveyed about their experiences, and conference notes and other documents are reviewed and analyzed. Of the 145 students served by the program during the spring and fall semesters of 2005, 30% have changed their major and started receiving advising from a college advisor, while an additional 43% continue to receive their

Table 10-2. Changes in group mean GPA and retention over time, Nursing majors, fall 2004 through fall 2005

Status	Fall 2004 (before program implementation)		Spring 2005			Fall 2005		
	Mean Term GPA	Mean Cum. GPA	No. of participants	Mean Term GPA	Mean Cum. GPA	No. of participants	Mean Term GPA	Mean Cum. GPA
Stayed Major	1.47	1.47	26	1.82	1.68	10	2.23	2.04
Changed Major	1.23	1.23	12	2.22	1.85	12	2.06	1.97
Withdrew			17			4		

advising through Student Academic Services (Atwood & Hutson, 2006; Hutson et al., 2006). In addition, students who have participated in the program report a greater sense of empowerment and of being in control of their academic situation after having participated in the program.

Academic Contracts with Students Returning from Dismissal

Program Description

At UNCG, students who have been dismissed for academic reasons may appeal for readmission after one year. In a fall 2006 pilot initiative, readmitted students were asked to sign a contract with Student Academic Services in which they committed to several advising sessions supplemented by short written assignments designed to help them identify personal strengths and interests, develop a personal academic recovery plan, and find sources of academic and personal support. These advising sessions emphasize the use of Appreciative Advising.

Results

Out of 18 academically dismissed students who were readmitted, 12 participated in the program. At the end of the fall 2006 semester, 90% of the participants in the program were eligible to continue in the spring 2007 semester and 58% had earned term GPAs of over 3.00. The mean GPA among participants was 2.86. In contrast, among students who did not participate, 33% were eligible to continue and their mean GPA was 1.29 (Hutson & Clark, 2007).

To further examine the impact of the program, two more indicators were used: cumulative GPA of participants over time and percentage of participants who earned good-standing status. Participants' average GPAs have been consistently higher than those who did not participate in the program (Figure 10-4), and as indicated in Figure 10-5, participants were far more likely to attain good standing than were nonparticipants.

Figure 10-4. Comparison of GPAs for participants and nonparticipants over time

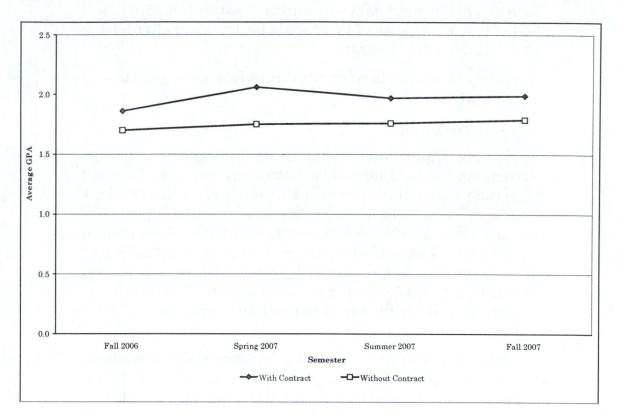

Figure 10-5. Percentage of dismissal contract participants in good standing

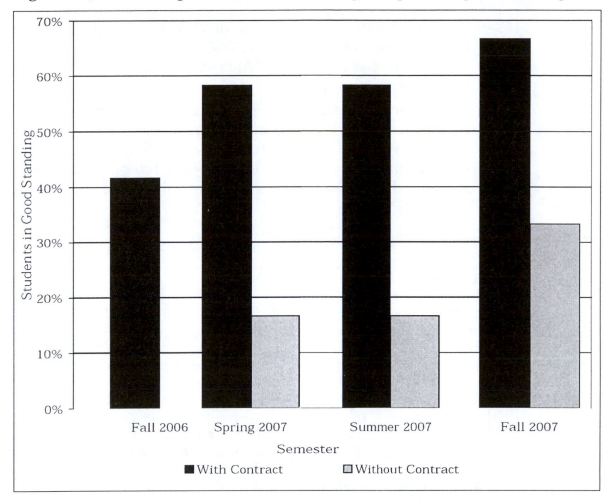

Because the pilot was successful, the university adopted a new policy requiring students who have been readmitted after academic dismissal to participate in the Appreciative Advising sessions that Student Academic Services provides (Hutson & Clark, 2007). In fall 2007, the first semester in which all formerly dismissed students were required to engage in contracts, 92% were able to continue after the first semester of readmittance (Dozier, Davis, Yang, Ross, & Hutson, 2008).

Features of Appreciative Advising across Programs

Various features of Appreciative Advising are highlighted in the programs mentioned above. Table 10-3 summarizes the key features and characteristics of Appreciative Advising implementation in each program.

Student Academic Services is in the process of exploring and experimenting with the implementation of Appreciative Advising in an early warning system as well as expanding the dismissal-recovery program and extending the SAS 100 program to any student who goes on probation at any point in her/his enrollment at UNCG.

Table 10-3. Appreciative Advising features in UNCG advising programs

Program	Appreciative Advising (AA) Components	Objectives
SAS 100	AA Inventory pre and post; Individual conferences using AAI and AA interview questions	measure student assets for academic success; facilitate student to leverage assets for enhanced academic attitude and strategies
UNS 101	SPA—Strengths, Purpose, Alignment	facilitate student transition into college life support student academic pursuit by aligning purpose with program strengths
Transfer Program	AA interview questions with individual advising sessions	identify student academic potentials and explore alternative majors; examine campus resources to support student individual academic pursuit
Dismissal Contracts	AA interview questions with individual advising sessions	facilitate student recovery to good academic standing; keep the momentum of student academic pursuit

Note. AAI is Appreciative Advising Inventory

Summary

A fully student-centered approach, Appreciative Advising guides students to uncover and appreciate the strengths and passions that they have brought with them to the institution. As illustrated here, Appreciative Advising is a powerful mechanism for increasing student retention and achievement. It can be infused into first-year experience programs, student retention programs, early warning systems, and more. The field of Appreciative Advising is still young, yet initial results at the UNCG indicate that it shows great promise.

CHAPTER 11

APPRECIATIVE ADVISING PROGRAM DEVELOPMENT AND ADMINISTRATION

When developing and administering Appreciative Advising–infused initiatives, program developers need to keep the Appreciative Advising principles in mind and

1. involve all stakeholders in the initiation of the program;

2. identify the strengths and resources available on campus;

3. discuss the vision, goals, and objectives of the program and their alignment with standards and accreditation criteria;

4. systematically plan for program administration;

5. provide ongoing support to encourage program advancement; and

6. discuss new challenges and set higher expectations for program improvement.

In this section, we discuss the strategies that we have employed at each of these phases of program development and administration.

Program Initiation

At the initiation stage of an Appreciative Advising program, the program developer should share the Appreciative Advising principles with all personnel involved and obtain input from various stakeholders to identify the needs of the program and those it will serve. Professional development workshops, local conferences, and program retreats provide forums to start conversations regarding Appreciative Advising and its application on campus. Whether considering adapting Appreciative Advising to existing programs or applying it to new programs, proponents of Appreciative Advising may want to consider the following aspects of the population who will benefit:

- characteristics of the student population;

- current advising needs of the students;

- existing programs supporting the advising needs of the students;

- purpose of the Appreciative Advising–infused program; and

- people, offices, or programs that may be impacted by this change.

Strengths and Resources Identification

To identify the proper strengths and resources for the development and administration of the program, developers need to examine the existing resources available and maximize the strengths of existing programs. Strengths-based environment scanning can be utilized to search for campus resources that meet the diverse needs of all students.

Adapted from the original model, which was used in business settings, environmental scanning in higher education includes both macro and micro elements. (For information on environmental scanning, see Morrison, 1992.) The following outline provides a model that an advising-program developer can use to structure the search for resources:

1. Macro scanning elements to consider
   a. Changing social expectations of college graduates
   b. Changing characteristics of Generation Y
   c. Social cultural structures of higher education settings
   d. Changing needs for academic advising to sustain and prepare college students for society

2. Micro scanning elements to consider
   a. Academic advising needs from college students' perspectives
   b. Academic advising needs from the perspectives of higher education administrators, faculty members, and staff
   c. Campus resources needed to support student academic success
   d. Office mission, responsibilities, and tasks to facilitate the overall campus efforts

Goals and Objectives Discussion

Every advising program displays espoused objectives in its description. However, without discussions on the connection of these objectives to their daily work, advisors have difficulty embracing and enacting the professed goals. Therefore, we engaged developers and instructors of the first-year seminar in the discussion of the program blueprint.

Through the blueprint, we mapped out objectives that correlate to the developmental and academic needs of the students who take the class. In this case, the course developers expressed concerns over the way the course would assist students in four primary areas: developing improved learning strategies, learning about campus, supporting their transition to college from high school, and becoming a part of the campus community. They also wanted to ensure that students used higher order thinking in this class. The blueprint in Table 11-1 indicates how the objectives aligned with the goals of the course.

Table 11-1. Blueprint of goals and objectives for Appreciative Advising program

Implementation Stage	Learning Strategies	Campus	Transition	Community
Recognize	effective time management skills	campus resources available UNCG's history, traditions, and connection to current experiences	the differences between high school and college and how to make the transition, including expectations of the faculty	leadership styles and opportunities to lead and serve diversity/multiculturalism and the importance of respecting others' backgrounds the effects of drug and alcohol abuse and the importance of general wellness
Apply	effective time management skills effective note taking, study, and test taking skills learning styles	campus resources available advising and registration process	knowledge of money management skills	leadership styles and opportunities to lead and serve
Evaluate	personal motivation and ability to develop and pursue personal goals Align their interests, strengths, and academic major with career path			

This blueprint could be expanded to include the assignments and activities for the course and how they correspond with the objectives.

The blueprint allowed us to incorporate the ideals and targets in the minds of both the program developers and administrators. The goals of the program were explicitly stated and interpreted from the beginning.

Strategic Planning

The program design is the foundation of the program proposal. At some point, the program will need to be pitched to someone or some group on campus whose interest or support will facilitate its implementation. The following is the core question list we used to guide our planning and proposal writing:

1. Program alignment with institution goals
   a. How can the impacted student population (or a subset of students) be described?
   b. What benefits support the mission of the institution?
   c. How are the benefits linked to the program?

2. Program process
   a. What is the "official" process for change?
   b. Do proposals for specific policy change go to a faculty senate or committee, a provost, or a chief academic officer? Who comprises the audience?
   c. Who is involved in conducting the program? Who is responsible?
   d. What is the time line for program development, administration, and evaluation?

3. Program impact
   a. Who is impacted by this initiative?
   b. What kind of changes and opportunities will the program create?
   c. How can stakeholders' questions about the need for change be best addressed?

Program Improvement

Not every university is a natural site for the Appreciative Advising mindset. The weight of research obligations, the pressure to create new knowledge, and the focused nature of the expertise that has been developed often conspire against an inclusive, expansive, contextualized way of knowing.

Each staff person in the office, along with a large represen-
tative sample of students, staff in partner offices, and faculty
members who have been impacted by advisors' work need to be
involved in the Appreciative Advising training and be informed
of the Appreciative Advising results and impacts. In the following
chapter, we will further discuss the framework and strategies
used in program evaluation for program improvement.

CHAPTER 12

APPRECIATIVE ADVISING
PROGRAM EVALUATION

The purposes for designing and conducting program evaluation while implementing Appreciative Advising are three-fold: a) to examine the impact of Appreciative Advising on the quality of advising on campus, b) to measure the effectiveness of the Appreciative Advising model on academic achievement and persistence, and c) to obtain feedback from all involved stakeholders for program improvement. To obtain ongoing feedback and track the outcomes of implementation, developers need to think about the program evaluation design as well as data collection and analysis methods while planning Appreciative Advising programming.

In this section, we introduce the use of the logic model in the program evaluation design and discuss data collection and analysis for the evaluation of Appreciative Advising. Finally, the use of Appreciative Advising evaluation in the professional development of advising offices is discussed.

When referring to evaluation, we speak specifically about collecting information to improve the Appreciative Advising programs and services that are offered. The focus of the evaluation is on the program rather than individual staff or student performance.

The Appreciative Advising mindset undergirds the program evaluation process. The model offers powerful, rigorous methods for understanding the performances of programs and services. These methods help developers identify both strengths and challenges from an appreciative perspective.

Evaluation Design

Over the past 5 years, we have been using the logic model in the evaluation of programs in the UNCG Student Academic Services Office; it is used to describe and illustrate the logical linkages among program inputs, activities, outputs, audiences, and short-, intermediate-, and long-term outcomes (W. K. Kellogg Foundation, 1998). The pictorial nature of the model and the logical reasoning required in planning make it a very useful tool in organizing efforts to evaluate programs. Successful implementation requires that the model be employed in the program development stage and that inputs are sought from multiple stakeholders. Table 12-1 lists the key stakeholders that program developers may want to consider in designing the evaluation plan.

Figure 12-1 illustrates a logic model design that captures important elements in the evaluation of Appreciative Advising model implementation. Program evaluators need to consider program input while keeping the ultimate long-term impact in mind. The logical steps in the middle suggest that program developers contemplate the proper use of assessment instruments

Table 12-1. Key stakeholders to consider when developing an Appreciative Advising program

Upstream Stakeholders		Community and administrators Student advising offices Faculty and instructors involved in academic advising program
Downstream Consumers	Immediate Recipients	Students Instructors Advisors
	Those Impacted Downstream	Other faculty members and staff across campus Parents and community Prospective students

Figure 12-1. Appreciative Advising (AA) evaluation logic model

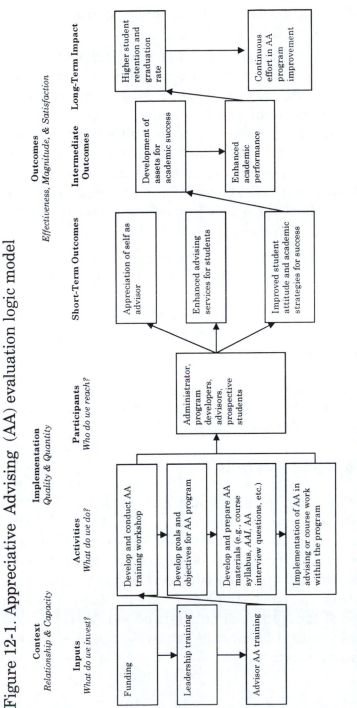

Note. AAI is *Appreciative Advising Inventory*

and associated data-gathering methods in measuring ongoing effectiveness of programs.

By following the logic model and identifying the key stake-holders, developers narrow down evaluation questions and refine their thinking about the purpose of the program and goals for it. Different programs have different foci and intents. Therefore, the general and specific research questions differ significantly from program to program. The following is an example of evalu-ation questions used in the evaluation of the implementation of Appreciative Advising in a first-year freshman seminar course; it focused on the short-term and immediate outcomes of the program (Hutson et al., 2006):

- What is the quality and effectiveness of the Appreciative Advising–infused UNS 101 course?

- What is the impact of the Appreciative Advising–infused UNS 101 course on student attitudes for academic success?

- What is the impact of the Appreciative Advising–infused UNS 101 course on student academic achievement and retention?

Data Collection and Analysis

Once the evaluation questions are identified, the data col-lection and analysis must be matched up with the evaluation queries to ensure that enough quality information is available to evaluate the program. Program developers must think through the data sources and analysis procedures early in the process so that the evaluation plan can be implemented simultaneously with implementation of the Appreciative Advising model. Table 12-2 is an example of a data collection and analysis plan designed to address evaluation questions.

Appreciative Advising Evaluation and Professional Development

In addition to informing the program developers, administrators, and other stakeholders, program evaluation results of Appreciative Advising model implementation could also be used to launch Appreciative Advising in advising offices.

Just as the Appreciative Advising process enhances self-knowledge and challenges advisors in their own academic and professional pursuits, the Appreciative Advising principles also facilitate positive cultural changes in advising offices across campus. Following the stages of Appreciative Advising offered for practice, advising office personnel can address the Disarm, Discover, Dream, Design, and Deliver phases collaboratively, and through utilization of the evaluation results, they can keep the institutional-level development momentum going through the Don't Settle stage.

Table 12-2. Indicators and measures for evaluation questions

Outcomes	Indicators	Measures
Quality and effectiveness of the UNS course	Student rating of the effectiveness of the course	First-Year-Initiative Survey
Impact of UNS course on student strategies for academic success	Student academic strategies for success	t-test of pre/post results for *Student Strategies for Success Survey*
Impact of UNS course on student academic achievement and retention	Students' term GPAs	t-test comparing student predicted GPA with student term GPA
	First-year college student retention rate	Comparison of retention rate between UNS participants and nonparticipants

Disarm. The collaborative design of the evaluation model as well as the data collection and analysis procedures call for various stakeholders to work together to establish common goals and objectives for the program. Such communication allows all parties involved in the development of the Appreciative Advising program to feel comfortable and involved from the beginning.

Discover. The ongoing evaluation results based on data collected from students, advisors, instructors, and administrators provide all stakeholders an opportunity to examine the strengths of advising services and resources. They can then plan to utilize them to provide better services for students with various backgrounds and advising needs.

Dream. Through discussions of evaluation results, office staff can modify the short-term, immediate, and long-term program outcomes such that they best suit institutional visions and dreams. The revision based on the edited "ideal impact" would lead to changes in outputs, activities, and inputs. Then, the implementation **Design** could be modified and corresponding support garnered to ensure that the new model is **Delivered.**

Don't Settle. The evaluation process is not a one-shot deal. The formative evaluation is only effective when improvement and development lead to continuous improvements. This ongoing data-based revising, redesigning, and redelivering of the advising program challenge all advisors and administrators to provide the best quality advising support to meet the changing needs of all students.

Summary

Systematic program evaluation in advising offices allows one to describe and verify the alignment between the missions, activities, and outcomes of the advising programs implemented, determine the effectiveness of such programs, and provide feedback to improve the delivery mechanism and facilitate administrative decision making. The application of the Appreciative Advising mindset in program evaluation involves all advisors as internal evaluators to identify and recognize their individual and group strengths and potentials. Through models provided in this chapter, Appreciative Advisors can develop effective evaluations of their Appreciative Advising programs.

Section IV:

The Future

CHAPTER 13

THE APPRECIATIVE ADVISING REVOLUTION REVISITED

Those who are revolutionized by the power of Appreciative Advising want to share their exciting discovery with co-workers. Yet, many who rush out to tell everyone in the office the multifaceted benefits of Appreciative Advising are often deafened by the resounding silence. A person who had not embraced the positive strength-based Appreciative Advising mindset might go back to the office feeling embarrassed, mad, and defeated. They might utter negative language such as, "Well, I gave it a try and it didn't work." Not the Appreciative Advising revolutionary: The one with an Appreciative Advising mindset will ask, "How can I use the Appreciative Advising model to support and challenge my colleagues to embrace the revolution?"

To encourage a paradigm shift, one must understand how others process change and how to sell change to others. John Kotter (1999, p. 31) stated that any change, positive or negative, produces "emotional turmoil" in people and that humans "can react very differently to change—from passively resisting it, to aggressively trying to undermine it, to sincerely embracing it." He warned leaders that resistance is commonly caused by one of four reasons: not wanting to lose something of value, not completely understanding the reasons for the change, concern that the change is not good for the unit, or a general apprehensiveness about change. Therefore, Appreciative Advising revolutionaries need to understand that by suggesting modifications to the status quo they are upsetting the very people they are trying to benefit from the transformation.

The notion of emotional turmoil may seem counter-Appreciative. However, the value of the Appreciative Advising approach is not merely that it leads people to focus on the positive aspects of situations and feel better about their experiences. Kenneth Gergen, in this 1978 paper "Toward Generative Theory," suggested that social science should provide ways to think about social structures and institutions and that these insights should lead to action. The theoretical nature of his argument is compelling, but the thought of putting his suggestions into practice causes discomfort to many.

The Appreciative approach can be generative in a number of ways. It is the quest for new ideas, images, theories, and models that liberate collective aspirations, alter the social construction of reality, and in the process, make available decisions and actions that had hitherto been unavailable or unimagined. When successful, an Appreciative implementation generates spontaneous, unsupervised, individual, group, and organizational action toward a better future. However, this dynamic causes upheaval: People operating in uncharted territory are out of their comfort zones.

John Kotter (1999, p. 7) proposed eight stages of change in his book *John D. Kotter on What Leaders Really Do*:

> In the most successful change efforts, people move through eight complicated stages in which they (1) create a sense of urgency, (2) put together a strong enough team to direct the process, (3) create an appropriate vision, (4) communicate that new vision broadly, (5) empower employees to act on the vision, (6) produce sufficient short-term results to give their efforts credibility and to disempower the cynics, (7) build momentum and use that momentum to tackle the tougher change problems, and (8) anchor the new behavior in organizational culture.

Kotter's first step is to create a sense of urgency. Probably the best way to create this urgency in colleagues involves presenting data related to the student population. What is the retention rate for all students, minority students, transfer students, and students on probation? Do student surveys indicate widespread student satisfaction with advising? What other data are available? If colleagues are concerned about the quality of advising, the Appreciative Advising proponent can direct them to the success experienced at UNCG.

If advising is viewed as a campus strength, staff members may not see the need to change. However, "While change is inevitable no one has ever advocated change for the sake of change. So don't. Instead, change with significant purpose" (Stavros, Cooperrider, & Kelly, 2003, p. 17).

The second step involves creating a team to help advocate implementing Appreciative Advising. Efforts will be much more effective (and less lonely) if a group of people advocate the switch to Appreciative Advising. However, the Appreciative Advising revolutionary knows to inspire others by using his/her own strengths: Advisors are accustomed to working one-on-one with students, so the leader of the revolution need only use those honed skills of communication to discuss Appreciative Advising principles or stages with a co-worker over lunch. The leader also knows that advisors possess that "deep-seated, insatiable, absolutely have-to-know, fanatical curiosity" (West & Anthony, 2005, p. 13), so they point their colleagues to www.appreciativeadvising. net and/or let them borrow this book. They plant the idea but give time for others to understand Appreciative Advising and its power. The change agent will likely need to engage in a number of one-on-one conversations, probably behind the scenes, about Appreciative Advising before the band of rebels presents the concept to the boss or the larger body of co-workers.

The team needs to develop a vision. The one-on-one conversations have probably led to a collective understanding of how Appreciative Advising can be incorporated into the unit. The team leader needs to ensure that the vision is based in the Appreciative Advising mindset because many of us have experienced or observed a basic human quality: that as people, we all act in ways that are consistent with our images of the future. All of us are profoundly affected by our prophecies, hopes, and aspirations. When we believe the future holds good things for us, we are courageous and more willing to take risks. When we believe the future is dark, we are more conservative, more guarded, more protective of what we have. (Trosten-Bloom & Whitney, 1999, p. 128)

Leaders do not implement cultural change. In fact, attempts to install a preferred culture generally have unintended consequences and often make things worse (Kotter & Heskett, 1992; Ogbonna, 1993). Instead, they permit or unleash culture change. Talking about the positive, as the Appreciative Advising revolutionary does, relates not solely to feelings but also to intent. The positive language comes from a cultivated Appreciative mindset (Bushe, 2001a, 2001b; Bushe & Pitman, 1991); that is, the positive reflects a focus of wanting more of a valued outcome (Bushe, 1995). Therefore, those who operate out of an Appreciative mindset recognize even the smallest amount of good and nurture it until they get more of it.

Tojo Thatchenkary and Carol Metzker (2006) have recently offered a theory of "appreciative intelligence," which is the capacity to see the potential that is trying to emerge in people and processes. Their expansive thinking about possibility is consistent with generative activity.

Kotter's fourth stage involves broadly communicating the vision. The leadership team must build on the strengths of its organization much as the team members do individually in Appreciative Advising. Some of the collected retention and student satisfaction data may be negative, but those with an Appreciative mindset strive to focus on the potential: "We're doing some things well, but we can always do better. I would like to present you with a cutting-edge advising theory called Appreciative Advising. It focuses on building on the best that our students bring to us so that we can partner with them to help them reach their full potentials." The presenter should bring this book because the theoretical infrastructure explained in it will lend credibility to efforts to persuade others.

Empowering people to act on the vision characterizes Kotter's fifth stage. The exact vision of how Appreciative Advising might work may not be fully embraced by everyone. However, by being flexible and letting others contribute their ideas to the process, the Appreciative team allows others to have ownership of this initiative, which is critical to implementation.

To engender ownership, the leader gives new team members assignments and the time, space, and freedom to carry out their assignments. Team members might be encouraged to coordinate a day-long office retreat focused on how to implement Appreciative Advising in the unit; start a series of discussions, based on this book, on the different phases of Appreciative Advising; or learn more about AI and/or Appreciative Advising through Internet searches and then report their findings back to the group.

The sixth stage of Kotter's model involves producing some short-term victories that give credibility to the movement and disempower cynics. Seth Godin (2003, p. 74) pointed out,

> If you're remarkable, then it's likely that some people won't like you. That's part of the definition of remarkable. Nobody gets unanimous praise— ever. The best the timid can hope for is to be unnoticed. Criticism comes to those who stand out.

Not everyone is going to buy into the vision, and the leader must take heart and stand steadfast in the conviction that Appreciative Advising will bring a positive revolution. When facing resistance, Appreciative Advisors can generate "a pocket of greatness" (Collins, 2007) in individual advising sessions, where they can control the paradigm being shared. To get the fire burning in others, they can assess student outcomes, collect stories of student success, and share them with others; however, they may be surprised (and delighted) to find that students have spread the word before the Appreciative Advisor gets the chance to do it.

In his seventh stage, Kotter advocates building on the momentum created earlier to overcome roadblocks. Appreciative Advising can be implemented in stages. For example, as suggested, the individual advising sessions provide a great place to start the revolution. Then, others can be persuaded to try a few of the behaviors that characterize the six stages of Appreciative Advising. Of course, offering support and challenge works for colleagues as well as for students: An enthusiastic leader can get colleagues to incorporate even more Appreciative Advising behaviors. An assessment should be conducted to reinforce the value of the changes.

Appreciative Advising brings positiveness, which leads to hope. The relationship between hope and generative images as well as the necessity of hope for generative action has been documented (Ludema, 2001). Many philosophers have pointed out that people will not collectively act to change the future if they do not have hope; in fact, some argue, change is born out of the discovery of common images for a better team, organization, or world. When advisors engage in the Discovery and Dream phases themselves, they replace cynicism with hope and then amazing generative outcomes abound.

Kotter's last stage involves anchoring positive behavior in the organizational culture. Appreciative Advising can be attached to culture through adoption of the Appreciative Advising mindset. Those who have a grateful outlook can gently remind complaining colleagues to reframe their interactions with difficult students. The language used to describe work, students, and offices has impact. Positive words lead to positive actions, so the level of whining and complaining needs to be curtailed.

Also, part of each staff meeting can be devoted to discussing this book and/or how the staff is positively impacting students' lives. The following question can be asked, "Who wants to share a story about an interaction where you felt that you had a positive impact on a student?" Celebrating the stories will help establish an Appreciative Advising mindset in the office.

As the staff adopts the Appreciative Advising model, the approach and philosophy should be highlighted in all materials: the unit's website, recruiting materials, and other handouts for students. Appreciative Advising is very student centered and sharing the philosophy with students in multiple venues (orientation, individual advising meetings, and written documents) will help Disarm students before they even arrive in the office.

Having a great idea does not guarantee that others will appreciate it. In this chapter we have focused on understanding the nature of how people process change and James Kotter's (1999) model for selling change. People and resources are available to the aspiring Appreciative Advising revolutionary (*you*) to help implement Appreciative Advising on campus.

Go to www.appreciativeadvising.net for further information on these resources.

> Each time a man stands up for an idea, or acts to improve the lot of others, or strikes out against injustice, he sends forth a tiny ripple of hope, and crossing each other from a million different centers of energy and daring, those ripples build a current that can sweep down the mightiest walls of oppression and resistance.
>
> Senator Robert Kennedy
> (Meyerson, 2001)

REFERENCES

Adams, G. (2008). *George Matthew Adams quotes*. Retrieved June 16, 2008, from www.brainyquote.com/quotes/quotes/g/georgematt132350. html

Angelou, M. (2006). *Maya Angelou quotes*. Retrieved June 12, 2008, from http://thinkexist.com/quotation/i-ve_learned_that_people_will_for-get_what_you/341107.html

Atwood, J. A., & Hutson, B. L. (2006, November). *When good programs go bad: Using formative evaluation to mitigate problems during program implementation*. Paper presented at the annual meeting of the American Evaluation Association, Portland, OR.

Baxter Magolda, M. B. (2001). *Making their own way: Narratives for transforming higher education to promote self-development*. Sterling, VA: Stylus Publishing.

Bloom, J. L. (in press). Moving on from college. In V. Gordon, W. R. Habley, & T. Grites (Eds.), *Academic advising: A comprehensive handbook* (2nd ed.). San Francisco: Jossey-Bass.

Bloom, J., & Martin, N. A. (2002). Incorporating appreciative inquiry into academic advising. *The Mentor: An Academic Advising Journal, 4*(3). Retrieved June 15, 2008, from www.psu.edu/dus/mentor/020829jb.htm

Bloom, J. L., Cuevas, A. E. P., Evans, C. V., & Hall, J. W. (2007, Fall). Graduate students' perceptions of outstanding graduate advisor characteristics. *NACADA Journal, 27*(2), 28–35.

Bobel, T. (2007, November). *Using the microskills hierarchy to communicate more effectively with students*. Paper presented at the Illinois Academic Advising Association Drive-In Conference, Bloomington, IL.

Buckingham, M. (2007a). *Go put your strengths to work: 6 Powerful steps to achieve outstanding performance*. New York: Free Press.

Buckingham, M. (Director). (2007b). *Trombone player wanted* [video]. Carlsbad, CA: The Marcus Buckingham Company.

Bushe, G. R. (1995). Advances in appreciative inquiry as an organization development intervention. *Organization Development Journal, 13*, 14–22.

Bushe, G. R. (2001a). *Clear leadership*. Palo Alto, CA: Davies-Black.

Bushe, G. R. (2001b). Five theories of change embedded in appreciative inquiry. In D. Cooperrider, P. Sorenson, D. Whitney, & T. Yeager (Eds.) *Appreciative Inquiry: An emerging direction for organization development*. Champaign, IL: Stipes.

Bushe, G. R., & Pitman, T. (1991). Appreciative process: A method for transformational change. *OD Practitioner, 23*(3), 1–4.

Carter-Scott, C. (2006). *Cheri Carter-Scott quotes*. Retrieved February 3, 2008, from http://thinkexist.com/quotation/remember-there_are_no_mistakes-only_lessons-love/341169.html

Chang, E. C. (1998). Hope, problem-solving ability, and coping in a college student population: Some implications for theory and practice. *Journal of Clinical Psychology, 54*(7), 953–62.

Chemers, M. M., Hu, L-T., & Garcia, B. F. (2001). Academic self-efficacy and first-year college student performance and adjustment. *Journal of Educational Psychology, 93*(1), 55–64.

Christman, P. (2005, October). *Narrative advising: A hands on approach to effective change*. Paper presented at the national conference of the National Academic Advising Association, Las Vegas, NV. Retrieved February 17, 2008, from www.nacada.ksu.edu/nationalconf/2005/handouts/S071H1.doc

Church, M. (2005). Integrative theory of academic advising: A proposition. *The Mentor: An Academic Advising Journal, 7*(1). Retrieved April 27, 2007, from www.psu.edu/dus/mentor/050615mc.htm

Collins, J. (2001). *Good to great: Why some companies make the leap and others don't*. New York: Harper Collins.

Collins, J. (2007). *Creating a pocket of greatness*. Retrieved February 25, 2008, from www.goodtogreat.com/audio/How%20do%20you%20do%20Stop%20Doing.mp3

Cooperrider, D. L. (1990). Positive image, positive action: The affirmative basis of organizing. In S. Srivastva & D. L. Cooperrider (Eds.), *Appreciative management and leadership: The power of positive thought and action in organizations* (pp. 91–125). San Francisco: .Jossey-Bass.

Cooperrider, D. L., & Whitney, D. (2000). A positive revolution in change: Appreciative inquiry. In D. L. Cooperrider, P.F. Sorensen, Jr., D. Whitney, & T. F. Yaeger (Eds.), *Appreciative inquiry: Rethinking human organization toward a positive theory of change* (pp. 3–27). Champaign, IL: Stipes.

Cooperrider, D. L., Sorenson, P. F., Whitney, D., & Yaeger, T. F. (Eds.). (2000). *Appreciative inquiry: Rethinking human organization toward a positive theory of change*. Champaign, IL: Stipes.

Council for the Advancement of Standards in Higher Education. (2005). *Academic advising: CAS standards and guidelines*. Retrieved April 20, 2008, from www.nacada.ksu.edu/Clearinghouse/Research_Related/CASStandardsForAdvising.pdf

Covey, S. R. (1989). *The seven habits of highly effective people*. New York: Simon & Schuster.

Covington, M. V. (1992). *Making the grade: A self-worth perspective on motivation and school reform*. New York: Cambridge University Press.

Crookston, B. B. (1994). A developmental view of academic advising as teaching. *NACADA Journal, 14*(2), 5–9. (Original work published 1972)

Crosby, R.P. (1992). *Walking the empowerment tightrope: Balancing management authority and employee influence*. King of Prussia, PA: Organization Design and Development.

Crosby, R. P. (1999). *The authentic leader: How authority and consensus intertwine*. Seattle, WA: Skaya.

Davis, B., Funderburk, N. S., & Hutson, B. L. (2008, May). *The assessment of a FYE program: Proactive evaluation methods*. Paper presented at the annual conference of Region III of the National Academic Advising Association, Columbia, SC.

Davis, S., Jenkins, G., & Hunt, R. (2002). *The pact: Three young men make a promise and fulfill a dream*. New York: Riverhead Books.

De Sousa, D. J. (2005). *What advisors can do* (Occasional Paper No. 11). National Survey of Student Engagement. Retrieved September 9, 2007, from http://nsse.iub.edu/institute/documents/briefs/DEEP%20Practice%20Brief%2011%20What%20Advisors%20Can%20Do.pdf

Downing, S. (2005). *On course: Strategies for creating success in college and in life* (4th ed.). Boston: Houghton Mifflin Company.

Dozier, J., Davis, B., Yang, S. M., Ross, R. A., & Hutson, B. L. (2008). *Student academic services: Annual review of programs*. Greensboro, NC: The University of North Carolina at Greensboro.

Emerald, D. (2006). *The power of TED: The empowerment dynamic*. Bainbridge Island, WA: Polaris.

Fiddler, M. B., & Alicea, M. (1996). Use of a collective narrative process to articulate practice-based advising competencies. *NACADA Journal, 16*(1), 14–20.

Flora, C. (2004). The once-over: Can you trust first impressions? [Electronic version]. *Psychology Today, 37*(3). Retrieved June 17, 2008, from www.psychologytoday.com/articles/pto-20040713-000004.html

Fortgang, L. B. (2007). *Mirror image coaching and consulting.* www.mirrorimagecoaching.com/philosophy.html

Fredrickson, B. L. (2001). The role of positive emotions in positive psychology: The broaden-and-build theory of positive emotions. *American Psychologist, 56*, 218–26.

Fredrickson, B. L. (2006). Unpacking positive emotions: Investigating the seeds of human flourishing. *Journal of Positive Psychology, 1*, 57–60.

Gay, G. (2000). *Culturally responsive teaching: Theory, research, & practice.* New York: Teachers College Press.

Gergen, K. (1978). Toward generative theory. *Journal of Personality and Social Psychology, 36*, 1344–60.

Glasser, W. (1986). *Choice theory in the classroom.* New York: Harper Perennial.

Glasser, W. (2000). *Counseling with choice theory.* New York: Harper Collins.

Godin, S. (2003). PURPLE COW: Transform your business by becoming remarkable. *Fast Company, 67,* 74.

Gouker, J., Hutson, B. L., Dozier, J., Mobley, K., Davis, B., & Ross, R. A. (2008, May). *When academics is not enough: Providing counseling to students on academic probation.* Paper presented at the annual conference of Region III of the National Academic Advising Association, Columbia, SC.

Habley, W. R., & Bloom, J. L. (2007). Giving advice that makes a difference. In G. L. Kramer (Ed.), *Fostering student success in the campus community* (pp. 171–92). San Francisco: Jossey-Bass.

Hagen, P. L. (2007). Narrative theory and academic advising. *Academic Advising Today, 30*(3), pp. 5, 19.

Heath, C., & Heath, D. (2007). *Made to stick: Why some ideas survive and some don't.* New York: Random House.

Hemwall, M. H., & Trachte, K. C. (1999). Learning at the core: Toward a new understanding of academic advising. *NACADA Journal, 19*(1), 5–11.

Henderson, J., & Henderson, R. (2007). *There's no such thing as public speaking*. New York: Penguin Group (USA).

Hossler, D., & Bean, J. P. (Eds.). (1990). *The strategic management of college enrollments*. San Francisco: Jossey-Bass.

Hutson, B. L. (2003). *Student Strategies for Success Survey*. Greensboro, NC: University of North Carolina at Greensboro.

Hutson, B. L. (2006). *Monitoring for success: Implementing a proactive probation program for diverse, at-risk college students*. Unpublished doctoral dissertation, University of North Carolina at Greensboro.

Hutson, B. L., & Atwood, J. A. (2006, November). *Outcome evaluation to support a freshman orientation program*. Paper presented at the annual meeting of the American Evaluation Association, Portland, OR.

Hutson, B. L., & Clark, J. A. (2007, May). *Reaching out to those who have been dismissed: An application of appreciative advising*. Poster presented at the annual conference of Region III of the National Academic Advising Association, Asheville, NC.

Hutson, B. L., Amundsen, S. A., & He, Y. (2005, April). *Monitoring for success: Implementing a proactive probation program for diverse, at-risk college students*. Paper presented at the annual meeting of the American Educational Research Association, Montreal, QC.

Hutson, B. L., He, Y., & Amundsen, S. A. (2006, November). *Evaluating the impact of appreciative advising across higher education institutions: A multi-site evaluation*. Poster presented at the annual meeting of the American Evaluation Association, Portland, OR.

Ivey, A. E., & Ivey, M. B. (2007). *Intentional interviewing and counseling: Facilitating client development in a multicultural society* (6th ed.). Pacific Grove, CA: Brooks/Cole-Thompson Learning.

Jones, D. (Director). (1999). *Everyday creativity* [video]. Zepher Cove, NV: Dewitt Jones Productions.

Kamphoff, C. S., Hutson, B. L., Amundsen, S. A., & Atwood, J. A. (2007). A motivational/empowerment model applied to students on academic probation. *Journal of College Student Retention: Research, Theory, and Practice, 8*(4), 397–412.

Kotter, J. P. (1999). *John P. Kotter on what leaders really do*. Boston: Harvard Business Review.

Kotter, J. P., & Heskett, J. L. (1992). *Corporate culture and performance*. New York: The Free Press.

Kuh, G., Kinzie, J., Schuh, J. H., & Whitt, E. J. (Eds.). (2005). *Student success in college: Creating conditions that matter*. San Francisco: Jossey-Bass.

Laing, R. D. (1967). *The politics of experience*. New York: Ballantine Books.

Light, R. (2001). *Making the most of college*. Cambridge, MA: Harvard University Press.

Lipman, D. (1995). *The storytelling coach: How to listen, praise and bring out people's best*. Little Rock, AR: August House.

Lowenstein, M. (1999). An alternative to the developmental theory of advising. *The Mentor: An Academic Advising Journal, 1*(4). Retrieved April 27, 2007, from www.psu.edu/dus/mentor/991122ml.htm

Ludema, J. (2001). From deficit discourse to vocabularies of hope: The power of appreciation. In D. Cooperrider, P. F. J. Sorensen, T. F. Yaeger, & D. Whitney (Eds.), *Appreciative inquiry: An emerging direction for organizational development* (pp. 265–87). Champaign, IL: Stipes.

Maslow, A. (1954). *Motivation and Personality*. New York: Harper.

McLagen, M., & Treisman, J. (Executive Producers). (2000). *Pay it forward* [Motion Picture]. United States: Warner Home Video.

Melander, E. R. (2002). The meaning of "student-centered" advising: Challenges to the advising learning community. *The Mentor: An Academic Advising Journal, 4*(4). Retrieved April 27, 2007, from www.psu.edu/dus/mentor/991122ml.htm

Meyerson, D. E. (2001). *Tempered radicals: How people use difference to inspire change at work*. Boston: Harvard Business School Press.

Monk, G., Winslade, J., Crocket, K., & Epston, D. (1997). *Narrative theory in practice: The archaeology of hope*. San Francisco: Jossey-Bass.

Morrison, J. L. (1992). Environmental scanning. In M. A. Whitely, J. D. Porter, & R. H. Fenske (Eds.), *A primer for new institutional researchers* (pp. 86–99). Tallahassee, FL: The Association for Institutional Research.

O'Banion, T. (1994). An academic advising model. *NACADA Journal, 14*(2), 10–16. (Original work published 1972)

Ogbonna, E. (1993). Managing organizational culture: Fantasy or reality? *Human Resource Management Journal, 3*, 42–54.

Orem, S. L., Binkert, J., & Clancy, A. L. (2007). *Appreciative coaching: A positive process for change*. San Francisco: Jossey-Bass

Patterson, K., Grenny, J., McMillan, R., & Switzler, A. (2002). *Crucial conversation: Tools for talking when stakes are high*. New York: McGraw-Hill.

Peterson, C. (2006). *Primer in positive psychology*. New York: Oxford University Press.

Positive Psychology Center. (2008). *Positive psychology center*. Retrieved April 30, 2008, from www.ppc.sas.upenn.edu/

Rath, T., & Clifton, D. O. (2004). *How full is your bucket? Positive strategies for work and life*. New York: Gallup Press.

Reiter, A. F. (2005). Meet Joe White: New UI president talks about leadership, goals and responsibility. *Illinois Alumni Magazine, 17*(5), 20–23.

Rolo, C. (2004). *An intervention for fostering hope, athletic and academic performance in university student-athletes*. Unpublished doctoral dissertation. Greensboro: The University of North Carolina at Greensboro.

Ruiz, D. M. (1997). *The four agreements: A practical guide to personal freedom*. San Rafael, CA: Amber-Allen Publishing.

Sanford, N. (1966). *Self and society: Social change and individual development*. New York: Atherton.

Sanford, N. (1968). *Where colleges fail: A study of student as person*. San Francisco: Jossey-Bass.

Search Institute. (2006). *The 40 developmental assets*. Retrieved April 28, 2008, from www.search-institute.org/assets/

Snyder, C. R., & Lopez, S. J. (2007). *Positive psychology: The scientific and practical explorations of human strengths*. Thousand Oaks, CA: Sage.

Snyder, C. R., Feldman, D. B., Shorey, H. S., & Rand, K. L. (2002, June). Hopeful choices: A school counselor's guide to hope theory. *Professional School Counseling, 5*(5), 298–307.

Snyder, C. R., Shorey, H. S., Cheavens, J., Pulvers, K. M., Adams, V. H., & Wiklund, C. (2002). Hope and academic success in college. *Journal of Educational Psychology, 94*(4), 820–26.

Snyder, C. R., Harris, C., Anderson, J. R., Holleran, S. A., Irving, L. M., Sigmon, S. T. et al. (1991). The will and the ways: Development and validation of an individual-differences measure of hope. *Journal of Personality and Social Psychology, 60*(4), 570–85.

Stavros, J., Cooperrider, D., & Kelly, D. L. (2003, November). Strategic inquire > appreciative intent: Inspiration to SOAR a new framework for strategic planning. *AI Practitioner*, 10–17.

Stickel, S. A., & Callaway, Y. L. (2007). *Neuroscience and positive psychology: Implications for school counselors.* (ERIC Document ED 498365)

Thatchenkary, T., & Metzker, C. (2006). *Appreciative intelligence.* San Francisco: Berret-Koehler.

Tichy, N. M. (2002). *The leadership engine: How winning companies build leaders at every level.* New York: Harper Collins.

Trosten-Bloom, A., & Whitney, D. (1999). Appreciative inquiry: The path to positive change. In M. K. Key (Ed.), *Managing change in healthcare: Innovative solutions for people-based organizations* (pp. 113–28). New York: McGraw-Hill.

Vygotsky, L. S. (1978). *Mind in society: The development of higher psychological processes.* Cambridge, MA: Harvard University Press.

Watkins, J. M., & Mohr, B. J. (2001). *Appreciative inquiry: Change at the speed of imagination.* San Francisco: Jossey-Bass/Pfeiffer.

West, S., & Anthony, M. (2005). *Your client's story: Know your clients and the rest will follow.* Chicago: Dearborn Trade Publishing.

Whitney, D., & Trosten-Bloom, A. (2003). *The power of appreciative inquiry: A practical guide to positive change.* San Francisco: Berrett-Koehler.

Wiggins, G., & McTighe, J. (2001). *Understanding by design.* New Jersey: Prentice-Hall.

W. K. Kellogg Foundation. (1998). *The W.K. Foundation evaluation handbook.* Battle Creek, MI: Author.

APPENDIX A

APPRECIATIVE ADVISING INVENTORY[1,2]

		Strongly Disagree	Disagree	Neither Disagree Nor Agree	Agree	Strongly Agree
1.	I am committed to being a life-long learner.	☐	☐	☐	☐	☐
2.	I am committed to earning a degree.	☐	☐	☐	☐	☐
3.	I attend all my classes.	☐	☐	☐	☐	☐
4.	College is preparing me for a better job.	☐	☐	☐	☐	☐
5.	I have a commitment to self-development and personal growth.	☐	☐	☐	☐	☐
6.	I have a strong desire to get good grades.	☐	☐	☐	☐	☐
7.	At the present time, I am actively pursuing my academic goals.	☐	☐	☐	☐	☐
8.	It is important to help others and I do so on a regular basis.	☐	☐	☐	☐	☐
9.	When challenged, I stand up for my beliefs and convictions.	☐	☐	☐	☐	☐

[1] The Developmental Assets® are used with permission by Search Institute.® Copyright © 1997, 2006 Search Institute, 615 First Avenue NE, Minneapolis, MN 55413; to learn more about Developmental Assets and to view the original framework, visit www.search-institute.org. All rights reserved.

[2] AAI development team members are Scott Amundsen, Jenny Bloom, Cathy Buyarski, Phil Christman, Amanda Cuevas, Linda Evans, Ye He, Bryant Hutson, Joe Murray, Claire Robinson, and Kaye Woodward.

		Strongly Disagree	Disagree	Neither Disagree Nor Agree	Agree	Strongly Agree
10.	I take personal responsibility for my actions and decisions.	☐	☐	☐	☐	☐
11.	I have a strong desire to make something of my life.	☐	☐	☐	☐	☐
12.	I'm good at planning ahead and making decisions.	☐	☐	☐	☐	☐
13.	I know and feel comfortable around people of different cultural, racial, and/or ethnic backgrounds.	☐	☐	☐	☐	☐
14.	I believe in myself and my abilities.	☐	☐	☐	☐	☐
15.	I have built positive relationships with my friends.	☐	☐	☐	☐	☐
16.	I feel that I have control over many things that happen to me.	☐	☐	☐	☐	☐
17.	I feel good about being a college student.	☐	☐	☐	☐	☐
18.	I feel positive about my future.	☐	☐	☐	☐	☐
19.	Right now I see myself as being pretty successful.	☐	☐	☐	☐	☐
20.	At this time, I am meeting the goals I have set for myself.	☐	☐	☐	☐	☐
21.	If I should find myself in a difficult situation, I could think of many ways to get out of it.	☐	☐	☐	☐	☐
22.	I can think of many ways to reach my current goals.	☐	☐	☐	☐	☐
23.	I feel that my family supports my educational pursuits.	☐	☐	☐	☐	☐
24.	I feel loved by my family.	☐	☐	☐	☐	☐
25.	I value my parents' advice.	☐	☐	☐	☐	☐

		Strongly Disagree	Disagree	Neither Disagree Nor Agree	Agree	Strongly Agree
26.	I know at least 3 people who work at my university that I can go to for advice and support.	☐	☐	☐	☐	☐
27.	It is important that I not let my professors or teachers down.	☐	☐	☐	☐	☐
28.	I participate in community activities.	☐	☐	☐	☐	☐
29.	Someone outside my family supports my educational pursuits.	☐	☐	☐	☐	☐
30.	My parents support my educational pursuits.	☐	☐	☐	☐	☐
31.	My close friends support my educational pursuits.	☐	☐	☐	☐	☐
32.	My university is a caring, encouraging place.	☐	☐	☐	☐	☐
33.	I feel valued and appreciated by my fellow students.	☐	☐	☐	☐	☐
34.	I have at least 2 adults in my life that model positive, responsible behavior.	☐	☐	☐	☐	☐
35.	My best friends model responsible behavior. They are a good influence on me.	☐	☐	☐	☐	☐
36.	I participate in activities on campus.	☐	☐	☐	☐	☐
37.	It is important for me to consider social expectations while making decisions.	☐	☐	☐	☐	☐
38.	I seek the opinions of my family when faced with major decisions.	☐	☐	☐	☐	☐
39.	I seek the opinions of my friends when faced with major decisions.	☐	☐	☐	☐	☐
40.	The values of my institution are consistent with my own.	☐	☐	☐	☐	☐

	Strongly Disagree	Disagree	Neither Disagree Nor Agree	Agree	Strongly Agree
41. I am working hard to be successful.	☐	☐	☐	☐	☐
42. I have good time management skills.	☐	☐	☐	☐	☐
43. I turn in all my assignments on time.	☐	☐	☐	☐	☐
44. I successfully balance my academic pursuits with my personal life.	☐	☐	☐	☐	☐

APPENDIX B

APPRECIATIVE ADVISING INVENTORY FOLLOW-UP QUESTIONS

Categories	Items	Advisor Questions
Commitment to Learning	1. I am committed to being a life-long learner. 2. I am committed to earning a degree. 3. I attend all my classes. 4. College is preparing me for a better job. 5. I have a commitment to self-development and personal growth. 6. I have a strong desire to get good grades. 7. At the present time, I am actively pursuing my academic goals.	• Tell me about a time when you felt motivated to do well in school. What was your motivation? • Tell me about a time when you felt that you were actively engaged in learning. How did you feel? What made you feel engaged? • Tell me about a time when you enjoyed doing class projects or assignments. How do you feel? Why do you think you enjoyed it? • Tell me about a time when you volunteered at your school? Why did you choose to do that? • Tell me about a time when you experienced academic success in college. Why do you consider that a success? What did you do to make it successful? Who helped you? • Describe what your ideal college life looks like. Why? • What impact will your college degree have on your life? How do you envision your life being different because of the degree?

| Positive Values | 8. It is important to help others and I do so on a regular basis.
9. When challenged, I stand up for my beliefs and convictions.
10. I take personal responsibility for my actions and decisions.
11. I have a strong desire to make something of my life. | • Tell me about a time when you helped out a person in your life.
• Tell me about a time when you stood up for your beliefs and convictions, even when it may not have been easy to do so.
• When was the last time that you handled a difficult situation well? What strategies did you utilize in handling it?
• What obstacles have you overcome to be successful as a college student here?
• How are you going to make the world a better place during your time on this planet?
• How are you going to make the campus a better place than you found it? What are your most important values? How do you live out these values? Who in your life was the most influential in helping you develop these values? |
| Social Competencies | 12. I'm good at planning ahead and making decisions.
13. I know and feel comfortable around people of different cultural, racial, and/or ethnic backgrounds.
14. I believe in myself and my abilities.
15. I have built positive relationships with my friends. | • Tell me about a time when you made a difficult decision that turned out well.
• Tell me about a time when you did a great job of planning ahead.
• Tell me about a time when you worked together with a person from a different cultural, racial, and/or ethnic background.
• What single accomplishment in your life has boosted your self-confidence the most?
• Tell me about a time when you went out of your way to build a relationship with a new person.
• What is the nicest thing that you have ever done for someone else?
• What is the nicest thing that one of your friends has ever done for you? |

Positive Identity		
	16. I feel that I have control over many things that happen to me.	• Tell me about a time when you faced a challenge but felt you had control over the outcome. In what ways did you exercise this control?
	17. I feel good about being a college student.	• What is the best part of being a college student?
	18. I feel positive about my future.	• Describe your life 5 and 10 years after graduation. Where will you live? What will your work/career be like? What is the role of family? How do you spend your leisure time?
	19. Right now I see myself as being pretty successful.	• Describe your biggest success to date.
	20. At this time, I am meeting the goals I have set for myself.	• Describe your biggest success in college. Why is this a success? What role did you play in making this a success?
	21. If I should find myself in a difficult situation, I could think of many ways to get out of it.	• Tell me a about a tough situation you have faced while in college and how you got out of it. What specific tools (e.g., behaviors, beliefs, support systems) did you use to get out of this situation?
	22. I can think of many ways to reach my current goals.	• Tell me about a current goal. What is one thing you have done in the past week/month to move toward reaching that goal? • Tell me about a current goal. What is your plan to achieve that goal? If this plan doesn't work, tell me about another way you could achieve this goal.

Support/Connectedness	23.	I feel that my family supports my educational pursuits.	• Can you share a specific instance when your family showed support of your educational pursuits?
	24.	I feel loved by my family.	• Other than financial, how do your parents take an active interest in your educational success?
	25.	I value my parents' advice.	• How would you describe your relationship with your parents?
	26.	I know at least 3 people who work at my university that I can go to for advice and support.	• Describe your parents' way of giving you advice. How do you typically respond to their advice?
	27.	It is important that I not let my professors or teachers down.	• If you were going to go to someone other than a parent for advice, who would that be?
	28.	I participate in community activities.	• Can you think of a person at your university to whom you could go and talk about life decisions? Career decisions? Personal decisions? Do you have a similar relationship with any other individuals at the university?
	29.	Someone outside my family supports my educational pursuits.	• Tell me about a positive relationship you have or have had with a professor at the university.
	30.	My parents support my educational pursuits.	• Explain how the values of your university are consistent with your own.
	31.	My close friends support my educational pursuits.	• Could you elaborate on your relationship with those closest to you at the university? How have you drawn support from each other?
			• In what kind of community activities are you involved? How do they make you feel strong?

| Empowerment | 32. My university is a caring, encouraging place.
33. I feel valued and appreciated by my fellow students.
34. I have at least 2 adults in my life that model positive, responsible behavior.
35. My best friends model responsible behavior. They are a good influence on me.
36. I participate in activities on campus. | • Tell me about a time when you felt that the university was a caring, encouraging place.
• Who are the two most positive, influential role models in your life? Why do you admire them?
• Tell me about a time when you saw one of your best friends model responsible behavior.
• What is the best activity in which you have participated on campus? Why?
• Tell me about a time when a fellow student helped you or someone else in a time of need?
• Who is your best friend? What do you admire most about this person?
• Tell me about a time that you have had a positive impact on another person's life.
• Tell me about a time when someone else has had a positive impact on or made a difference in your life.
• What new club or activity on campus would you be inclined to join? Why?
• What new special interest club on campus would you initiate? Why? How would you go about starting such a club?
• What is one thing that you could do to help the university become a more caring, encouraging place?
• When you graduate, what do you hope will be your legacy? What do you hope to take with you? |

Boundaries & Expectations	37. It is important for me to consider social expectations while making decisions.	• Tell me about a time when you think you made the right decision. How did you do that? Who did you talk with before making that decision?
	38. I seek the opinions of my family when faced with major decisions.	• Tell me about a time when you were encouraged to do something in which you were successful. Who encouraged you? How?
	39. I seek the opinions of my friends when faced with major decisions.	• Describe someone you consider your role model. Why do you consider him/her as your role model?
	40. The values of my institution are consistent with my own.	• Tell me about a time when the rules set by your family or school helped you make the right decision.
		• Tell me about a time when your friends had a positive impact on your decision making.

| Constructive Use of Time | 41. I am working hard to be successful.

42. I have good time management skills.

43. I turn in all my assignments on time.

44. I successfully balance my academic pursuits with my personal life. | • Tell me about a time when going the extra mile paid off for you.

• When was the last time that you were really excited about an event? What was exciting about it?

• Tell me about a time when you did an excellent job prioritizing tasks. How did you do it? How did you go about determining what was most important?

• Tell me about a time when you came through for someone (individual or group). What did you do and how did you do it? How did this make you feel?

• Describe the types of people with whom you work best. Give me a specific example involving positive collaboration.

• Who brings out the best in you?

• Name the hardest working person you know. Explain in detail what separates her/him from the pack.

• Tell me about a project or activity that made you lose track of time; that is, you spent hours upon hours on the activity without even thinking about it.

• Tell me about a time when you worked on a successful project that required a great deal of planning. How did you make it happen? Who were the key players?

• What is the best time of day for you to get things done?

• Tell me about a tough deadline that you were able to meet. How did you do it? Who were the key players? |

The Developmental Assets® are used with permission by Search Institute®. Copyright © 1997, 2006 Search Institute, 615 First Avenue NE, Minneapolis, MN 55413; To learn more about Developmental Assets and to view the original framework, visit www.search-institute.org. All rights reserved.

AAI development team members are Scott Amundsen, Jenny Bloom, Cathy Buyarski, Phil Christman, Amanda Cuevas, Linda Evans, Ye He, Bryant Hutson, Joe Murray, Claire Robinson, and Kaye Woodward.

FREQUENTLY ASKED QUESTIONS

As more people learn about Appreciative Advising, the more questions we are asked. Here are some responses to some of the most frequently asked questions.

1. What is the difference between appreciative inquiry (AI) and Appreciative Advising?

> *AI is an organizational development process or philosophy that describes the individual's relationship to the organizational system. David Cooperrider developed the concept, which is commonly used to enhance organizational effectiveness. AI focuses on the organization.*

> *Appreciative Advising depicts an advising model with a focus on individual development. It draws on the basic assumptions of AI in that strengths are considered the bases of solutions. A reciprocal process, Appreciative Advising emphasizes the quality of the contextualized interactions between advisors and students. Rather than focusing on organizational effectiveness, Appreciative Advising provides a positive mindset for individual growth. The outcomes include more efficient services provided by the institution to the individual student.*

> *AI describes how individuals contribute to the improvement of the organization; Appreciative Advising illustrates a mutually beneficial relationship between a student and an advisor.*

2. How do I implement Appreciative Advising when I only have 15 to 30 minutes with each student?

While more contact time could potentially enhance the rapport and strengthen the relationship between the advisors and the students, Appreciative Advising lends itself to interactions limited to short time frames. The ultimate goal of Appreciative Advising, to generate the Appreciative mindset in the student throughout the interactions, relies on well-trained advisors who embrace the Appreciative mindset themselves. Time constraints do not alter the mindset.

Advisors can strategically select one or two phases of Appreciative Advising for implementation in each session. In offices where several advisors work with one student, collaboration and an advising log to track student interactions and profiles will ensure that the tenets of the mindset are communicated. Through self-professional development and cooperation among themselves, advisors can engage students in Appreciative Advising in 15 to 30 minute sessions.

3. Can I implement one or two of the Appreciative Advising phases?

Yes. You can implement one or two of the Appreciative Advising phases in a session. While it is important to build relationships with students through Disarm and to understand students' backgrounds and needs through Discover, Appreciative Advising phases are not designed to be followed in a linear fashion. Instead, several phases may need to be repeated before the Appreciative Advisor can move to the next stage. When implementing one or two of the Appreciative Advising phases at one session with a student, the Appreciative Advisor must be clear about the goals for the particular session, and the student must understand the goals and the process. In other words, Appreciative Advisors must be candid about the purposes of the sessions from the beginning, and follow-up sessions need to be planned to complete the Appreciative Advising model for effective academic planning and support.

4. Which groups of students benefit from Appreciative Advising?

Appreciative Advising can be adopted and used with all groups of students. In this book, we describe the use of Appreciative Advising with individuals and those in groups. It can also be applied in advising-based courses such as first-year experience courses, transfer student orientations, and at-risk student interventions.

5. As a new advisor in the field, where do I start with the Appreciative Advising model?

As we stated at the beginning of Section II, we believe that advisors start with themselves when implementing the Appreciative Advising model. Without sufficient self-knowledge, advisors cannot implement any component of Appreciative Advising because it involves the development of an Appreciative habit of mind. The strategies recommended in this book as listed in the Tool Boxes for each phase provide new (and experienced) advisors with concrete steps to start with the Appreciative mind-set formation. However, advisors need to be patient with themselves and to set a pace that works the best for them. Starting with a peer and conducting some guided peer coaching may facilitate the process.

6. How do we start to adopt Appreciative Advising in our advising office on campus?

To adopt Appreciative Advising beyond individual advisors, we recommend introducing the concepts through book clubs, professional development efforts, or discussions with peers. Program developers must embed the evaluation effort from the beginning of implementation. The ongoing evaluation results provide formative feed-

back to program managers and facilitate the adaptation and modification of Appreciative Advising.

7. Where can I learn more about conducting program evaluations?

Great resources regarding program evaluation strategies and techniques are available via the Internet. The W.K. Kellogg Foundation (www.wkkf.org) has a number of resources on designing and conducting program evaluations that can be downloaded for free. The W. K. Kellogg Foundation Evaluation Handbook, *which emphasizes that evaluation should be a relevant and useful program tool that supports programming, makes a good starting reference.*

The Evaluation Center at Western Michigan University (www.wmich.edu/evalctr), the American Evaluation Association (www.eval.org), and www.evaluationwiki.org also provide information about different models for conducting evaluation. Some good print resources include E. Jane Davidson's Evaluation Methodology Basics: The Nuts and Bolts of Sound Evaluation (Sage Publications, 2004), Jody Fitzpatrick, James Sanders, and Blaine Worthen's Program Evaluation: Alternative Approaches and Practical Guidelines *(Allyn & Bacon, 2003), and Hallie Preskill and Tessie Tzavaras Catsambas'* Reframing Evaluation through Appreciative Inquiry *(Sage Publications, 2006).*

Experts may be found among the faculty and in the institutional research office. These colleagues can become part of the Appreciative Advising revolution too!

8. What are some other resources regarding Appreciative Advising?

Check out our website: www.appreciativeadvising.net. Share stories and network with other Appreciative Advisors in the field.